EXCITING
EXTRA
ONLINE
RESOURCES
INCLUDED

Kaplan Publishing are constantly finding new ways to make a difference to your studies and our exciting online resources really do offer something different to AAT students looking for exam success.

FOR THE FIRST TIME, KAPLAN'S AAT TEXTS COME WITH FREE EN-gage ONLINE RESOURCES SO THAT YOU CAN STUDY ANYTIME, ANYWHERE

Having purchased this Kaplan Text, you have access to the following online study materials:

- An online version of the Text
- Fixed Online Tests with instant answers

How to access your online resources

- **Kaplan Financial students** will already have a Kaplan EN-gage account and these extra resources will be available to you online. You do not need to register again, as this process was completed when you enrolled. If you are having problems accessing online materials, please ask your course administrator.
- **If you purchased through Kaplan Flexible Learning or via the Kaplan Publishing website** you will automatically receive an e-mail invitation to Kaplan EN-gage online. Please register your details using this e-mail to gain access to your content. If you do not receive the e-mail or book content, please contact Kaplan Flexible Learning.
- **If you are already a registered Kaplan EN-gage user** go to www.EN-gage.co.uk and log in. Select the 'add a book' feature and enter the ISBN number of this book and the unique pass key at the bottom of this card. Then click 'finished' or 'add another book'. You may add as many books as you have purchased from this screen.
- **If you are a new Kaplan EN-gage user** register at www.EN-gage.co.uk and click on the link contained in the e-mail we sent you to activate your account. Then select the 'add a book' feature, enter the ISBN number of this book and the unique pass key at the bottom of this card. Then click 'finished' or 'add another book'.

Your Code and Information

This code can only be used once for the registration of one book online. This registration will expire when the final sittings for the examinations covered by this book have taken place. Please allow one hour from the time you submitted your book details for us to process your request.

HucG-EdAd-twCP-3SEk

Please be aware that this code is case-sensitive and you will need to include the dashes within the passcode, but not when entering the ISBN. For further technical support, please visit www.EN-gage.co.uk

INDIRECT TAX

Qualifications and Credit Framework

Level 3 Diploma in Accounting

British Library Cataloguing-in-Publication Data

A catalogue record for this book is available from the British Library.

Published by
Kaplan Publishing UK
Unit 2, The Business Centre
Molly Millars Lane
Wokingham
Berkshire
RG41 2QZ

ISBN 978-0-85732-218-0

Printed in Great Britain by WM Print Ltd, Walsall.

We are grateful to the Association of Accounting Technicians for permission to reproduce past assessment materials and example tasks based on the new syllabus. The solutions to past answers and similar activities in the style of the new syllabus have been prepared by Kaplan Publishing.

We are grateful to HM Revenue and Customs for the provision of tax forms, which are Crown Copyright and are reproduced here with kind permission from the Office of Public Sector Information.

Information reproduced from the VAT Guide 700 is also subject to Crown Copyright.

KAPLAN PUBLISHING

CONTENTS

STUDY TEXT AND WORKBOOK

INTRODUCTION

HOW TO USE THESE MATERIALS

These Kaplan Publishing learning materials have been carefully designed to make your learning experience as easy as possible and to give you the best chance of success in your AAT assessments.

They contain a number of features to help you in the study process.

The sections on the Unit Guide, the Assessment and Study Skills should be read before you commence your studies.

They are designed to familiarise you with the nature and content of the assessment and to give you tips on how best to approach your studies.

STUDY TEXT

This study text has been specially prepared for the revised AAT qualification introduced in July 2010.

It is written in a practical and interactive style:

- key terms and concepts are clearly defined

- all topics are illustrated with practical examples with clearly worked solutions based on sample tasks provided by the AAT in the new examining style

- frequent practice activities throughout the chapters ensure that what you have learnt is regularly reinforced

- 'pitfalls' and 'examination tips' help you avoid commonly made mistakes and help you focus on what is required to perform well in your examination.

- clear advice as to which practice activities can be completed is given at the end of each chapter

WORKBOOK

The workbook comprises:

A question bank of practice activities with solutions, to reinforce the work covered in each chapter.

The questions are divided into their relevant chapters and students may either attempt these questions as they work through the textbook, or leave some or all of these until they have completed the textbook as a final revision of what they have studied

ICONS

The study chapters include the following icons throughout.

They are designed to assist you in your studies by identifying key definitions and the points at which you can test yourself on the knowledge gained.

 Definition

These sections explain important areas of Knowledge which must be understood and reproduced in an assessment

 Example

The illustrative examples can be used to help develop an understanding of topics before attempting the activity exercises

 Activity

These are exercises which give the opportunity to assess your understanding of all the assessment areas.

 Test your knowledge

At the end of each chapter these boxes will direct you to the Practice Activities that you can attempt after studying the chapter.

KAPLAN PUBLISHING

UNIT GUIDE

Indirect tax is divided into two units but for the purposes of assessment these units will be combined.

Principles of VAT (Knowledge)

2 credits

Preparing and Completing VAT returns (Skills)

2 credits

Purpose of the units

The AAT has stated that this unit is designed to ensure that learners can understand basic VAT regulations, accurately complete VAT returns and communicate VAT information to relevant people.

As VAT is subject to specific and detailed regulations, the learner should be able to seek guidance from relevant sources, process what is found and communicate this to others.

Learning objectives

On completion of these units the learner will be:

- able to deal with the most commonly occurring VAT issues in a business. Although some basic knowledge will be expected, the emphasis is not so much on recall as on awareness and understanding

- aware that regulations exist and know how to find the information to ensure that the business complies with the regulations and avoids surcharges and penalties

- able to extract information from the relevant source and, using their knowledge and understanding, apply the rules to the given situations

- aware of registration requirements and the existence of a variety of schemes with different requirements to suit businesses with different needs

- able to calculate VAT correctly and use an accounting system to extract the figures required to complete the VAT return

- aware of the special circumstances that require particular attention and be able to deal with errors and changes in the VAT rate, as well as being able to communicate on VAT issues with people inside and outside the business

Learning Outcomes and Assessment criteria

The unit consists of three learning outcomes, one for Knowledge and two for Skills, which are further broken down into Assessment criteria. These are set out in the following table with Learning Outcomes in bold type and Assessment criteria listed underneath each Learning Outcome. Reference is also made to the relevant chapter within the text.

Knowledge

To perform this unit effectively you will need to know and understand the following:

		Chapter
1	**Understand VAT regulations**	
1.1	Identify sources of information on VAT	1
1.2	Explain the relationship between the organisation and the relevant government agency	1
1.3	Explain the VAT registration requirements	2
1.4	Identify the information that must be included on business documentation of VAT registered businesses	3
1.5	Recognise different types of inputs and outputs	1, 3, 6
1.6	Identify how different types of supply are classified for VAT purposes	1, 6

- standard supplies

- exempt supplies

- zero rated supplies

- imports

- exports

		Chapter
1.7	Explain the requirements and the frequency of reporting for the following VAT schemes	4

- annual accounting
- cash accounting
- flat rate scheme
- standard scheme

1.8	Recognise the implications and penalties for the organisation resulting from failure to abide by VAT regulations including the late submission of VAT returns	5

Skills

To perform this unit effectively you will need to be able to do the following.

		Chapter
1	**Complete VAT returns accurately and in a timely manner**	
1.1	Correctly identify and extract relevant data for a specific period from the accounting system	6
1.2	Calculate accurately relevant inputs and outputs	1, 3, 6

- standard supplies
- exempt supplies
- zero rated supplies
- imports
- exports

1.3	Calculate accurately the VAT due to, or from, the relevant tax authority	6
1.4	Make adjustments and declarations for any errors or omissions identified in previous VAT periods	5, 6
1.5	Complete accurately and submit a VAT return within the statutory time limits along with any associated payments	4, 6

Delivery guidance

The AAT have provided delivery guidance giving further details of the way in which the unit will be assessed.

Principles of VAT – Understand VAT regulations

1.1 Identify sources of information on VAT

- Extract information from relevant sources.

1.2 Explain the relationship between the organisation and the relevant government authority. Understanding that:

- HMRC is a government body entitled to require organisations to comply with VAT regulations in relation to registration, record keeping, submission of returns, etc.

- VAT is a tax on consumer expenditure.

- it is advisable to get written confirmation from HMRC about issues on which doubt may arise as to the correct treatment.

- HMRC are entitled to inspect VAT records.

1.3 Explain the VAT registration requirements

- The registration threshold and when registration becomes compulsory.

- Circumstances in which voluntary registration may be beneficial to the business.

- Awareness of circumstances when deregistration may be appropriate, and the deregistration threshold.

- Which records must be kept and for how long.

1.4   Identify the information that must be included on business documentation of VAT- registered businesses

- And by implication information that is not required.

- Including less detailed VAT invoices and VAT receipts, and invoicing for zero rated and exempt supplies.

- Tax points – basic and actual, including where payment is in advance of supply or invoice is after the supply, but not continuous supply. The importance of tax points for determining eligibility for schemes, correct rate of VAT, and including figures on the VAT return.

- Time limits for VAT invoices including the 14-day rule.

- Rounding rules.

1.5   Recognise different types of inputs and outputs

- What are inputs and outputs, and what are input and output tax?

- How to treat different types of inputs and outputs in preparing a VAT return, including proforma invoices.

- the implication of the difference between zero rated and exempt supplies with respect to reclaiming input VAT should be recognised.

1.6   Identify how different types of supply are classified for VAT purposes

- standard supplies

- exempt supplies

- zero rated supplies

- imports

- exports

- No knowledge required of the detail of which specific items fall into each category.

- The basics of partial exemption, including an awareness of the de minimis limit that enables full recovery of input VAT for businesses with mixed exempt and taxable supplies. Calculations will not be required.

1.7   Explain the requirements and the frequency of reporting for the following VAT schemes

- annual accounting

- cash accounting

- flat-rate scheme

- standard scheme

- be able to explain in broad terms the way in which each scheme works and the situations in which an organisation would be likely to use one.

- know the effect of each scheme on the frequency of VAT reporting and payments.

1.8 Recognise the implications and penalties for the organisation resulting from failure to abide by VAT regulations including the late submission of VAT returns

The main principles of the enforcement regime, but not the fine detail.

- What triggers a surcharge liability notice. Will not be expected to know how the amount of the surcharge is calculated, or what happens if a further default arises in the surcharge period, etc.

- Penalties - awareness of fines and that evasion of VAT is a criminal offence.

Preparing and completing VAT returns

Complete VAT returns accurately and in a timely manner

1.1 Correctly identify and extract relevant data for a specific period from the accounting system

Learners will be expected to extract relevant net and VAT figures from the accounting system

- sales day book

- purchases day book

- cash book

- petty cash book

- journal

- general ledger accounts for sales, purchases, input VAT, output VAT.

1.2 Calculate accurately relevant inputs and outputs

- Using the basic rounding rule (rounding down total VAT to the nearest penny) calculate correctly the VAT and input and output figures for

  – Standard supplies

  – Exempt supplies

– Zero rated supplies

– Imports

– Exports

– The detailed rounding rules based on lines of goods and services and tax per unit or article are not required.

- *No knowledge required of the detail of which specific items fall into each category of standard, exempt and zero rated.*

- Be able to calculate VAT from net sales amounts at different rates of VAT, including cases when a settlement discount is offered.

- Be able to calculate the amount of VAT arising when given either the gross amount or the net amount of a supply.

- Know in broad terms how imports and exports, and their related VAT, are treated on a VAT return, including the significance of the EC.

- Know that exports are normally zero rated.

- Correctly account for VAT on business entertainment, sales and purchases of cars and vans and deposits or advance payments.

- Be aware of fuel scale charges and the effect on the total VAT payable/reclaimable (but no calculations).

1.3 Calculate accurately the VAT due to, or from, the relevant tax authority. In respect of:

- Transactions in the current period.

- Adjustments for bad debt relief.

1.4 Make adjustments and declarations for any errors or omissions identified in previous VAT periods

- The errors or omissions will be given.

- Identify whether the error or omission can be corrected on the current VAT return by identifying the threshold at which errors must be declared and the timescale during which corrections can be made.

- Apply the correct treatment.

- How to report an error that cannot be corrected on the current VAT return.

1.5 Complete accurately and submit a VAT return within the statutory time limits along with any associated payments

- Knowledge of what the time limits are, including those relating to non-standard schemes.

- Accurate calculation of the VAT due to, or from, HMRC, both in respect of transactions in the current period and also in relation to errors and omissions identified from previous periods.

  Transactions include sales and purchase invoices and credits, cash payments and receipts, petty cash payments.

- Complete a VAT return (VAT 100, paper or online version); Boxes 1 to 9.

- Be aware that most businesses will need to submit the VAT return and pay online.

- Understand that the balance on the VAT control account should agree to the figure on the VAT return and provide explanations for any difference.

Communicate VAT information

2.1 Inform managers of the impact that the VAT payment may have on the company cash flow and financial forecasts

- Know the time limits within which payment must be made under various schemes.

- Communicate this via standard communication methods such as emails.

2.2 Advise relevant people of the impact that any changes in VAT legislation, including the VAT rate, would have on the organisation's recording systems

- Basic understanding of the implication of a change in the VAT rate on the organisation using either manual or computerised systems.

- Basic understanding of who would need to be informed and why.

- Advise relevant people by email or other appropriate means.

2.3 Communicate effectively with the relevant tax authority when seeking guidance

- Using letters.

THE ASSESSMENT

The format of the assessment

The assessment will be divided into two sections comprising of six tasks.

Section 1:

There are five short-answer tasks assessing the learner's knowledge of the principles of VAT and their ability to understand and interpret VAT guidance given to them.

Some simple calculations will be required.

A number of the tasks will be multiple choice or true / false statements.

Section 2:

There will be one task. This will be the completion of a VAT return from information extracted from the accounting system, followed by a short piece of communication to an internal or external person.

The assessment material will normally be provided by the AAT, delivered online and assessed locally. If additional reference material is required, details will be provided in advance of the assessment. Learners will be required to demonstrate competence in both sections of the assessment.

Time allowed

The time allowed for this assessment is **90 minutes.**

Pass mark

The pass mark is 70%.

STUDY SKILLS

Preparing to study

Devise a study plan

Determine which times of the week you will study.

Split these times into sessions of at least one hour for study of new material. Any shorter periods could be used for revision or practice.

Put the times you plan to study onto a study plan for the weeks from now until the assessment and set yourself targets for each period of study – in your sessions make sure you cover the whole course, activities and the associated questions in the workbook at the back of the manual.

If you are studying more than one unit at a time, try to vary your subjects as this can help to keep you interested and see subjects as part of wider knowledge.

When working through your course, compare your progress with your plan and, if necessary, re-plan your work (perhaps including extra sessions) or, if you are ahead, do some extra revision / practice questions.

Effective studying

Active reading

You are not expected to learn the text by rote, rather, you must understand what you are reading and be able to use it to pass the assessment and develop good practice.

A good technique is to use SQ3Rs – Survey, Question, Read, Recall, Review:

1   Survey the chapter

   Look at the headings and read the introduction, knowledge, skills and content, so as to get an overview of what the chapter deals with.

2   Question

   Whilst undertaking the survey ask yourself the questions you hope the chapter will answer for you.

3   Read

Read through the chapter thoroughly working through the activities and, at the end, making sure that you can meet the learning objectives highlighted on the first page.

4   Recall

At the end of each section and at the end of the chapter, try to recall the main ideas of the section / chapter without referring to the text. This is best done after short break of a couple of minutes after the reading stage.

5   Review

Check that your recall notes are correct.

You may also find it helpful to re-read the chapter to try and see the topic(s) it deals with as a whole.

Note taking

Taking notes is a useful way of learning, but do not simply copy out the text.

The notes must:

- be in your own words
- be concise
- cover the key points
- well organised
- be modified as you study further chapters in this text or in related ones.

Trying to summarise a chapter without referring to the text can be a useful way of determining which areas you know and which you don't.

Three ways of taking notes

1   Summarise the key points of a chapter

2   Make linear notes

A list of headings, subdivided with sub-headings listing the key points.

If you use linear notes, you can use different colours to highlight key points and keep topic areas together.

Use plenty of space to make your notes easy to use.

3   Try a diagrammatic form

The most common of which is a mind map.

To make a mind map, put the main heading in the centre of the paper and put a circle around it.]

Draw lines radiating from this to the main sub-headings which again have circles around them.

Continue the process from the sub-headings to sub-sub-headings.

Highlighting and underlining

You may find it useful to underline or highlight key points in your study text – but do be selective.

You may also wish to make notes in the margins.

materials.

Further reading

In addition to this text, you should also read the "Student section" of the "Accounting Technician" magazine every month to keep abreast of any guidance from the examiners.

VAT REFERENCE INFORMATION

Note:

In your assessment you may be provided with additional reference information.

This information is provided for use in this Study text.

Standard rate of VAT	17.5%
VAT fraction (standard rated)	17.5/117.5
(often simplified to 7/47)	
Annual registration limit	£68,000
De – registration limit	£66,000
Cash Accounting:	
Turnover threshold to join scheme	£1,350,000
Turnover threshold to leave scheme	£1,600,000
Annual Accounting:	
Turnover threshold to join scheme	£1,350,000
Turnover threshold to leave scheme	£1,600,000
Flat rate scheme:	
Annual taxable turnover limit (excluding VAT) to join scheme	£150,000
Annual total income (including VAT) to leave scheme	£225,000

Introduction to VAT

1

Introduction

This chapter introduces some of the basic ideas of value added tax (VAT), which is the only tax studied in this paper on indirect tax.

This unit requires you to have knowledge of VAT rules, to be able to prepare VAT returns and be able to communicate VAT issues to the relevant people within an organisation.

KNOWLEDGE

Identify sources of information on VAT (1.1)

Explain the relationship between the organisation and the VAT authorities (1.2)

Recognise different types of inputs and outputs (1.5)

Identify how different types of supply are classified for VAT purposes (1.6)

SKILLS

Calculate accurately relevant inputs and outputs (1.2)

Communicate effectively with the relevant tax authority when seeking guidance (2.3)

CONTENTS

1 Introduction
2 Types of supply
3 Recovery of input tax
4 Output tax
5 Sources of information
6 HM Revenue and Customs

1 Introduction

1.1 What is VAT?

VAT is:

- an indirect tax,
- charged on most goods and services supplied within the UK,
- borne by the final consumer, and
- collected by businesses on behalf of HM Revenue and Customs.

VAT is an indirect tax because it is paid indirectly when you buy most goods and services, rather than being collected directly from the taxpayer as a proportion of their income or gains.

VAT is charged by **taxable persons** when they make **taxable supplies** in the course of their business. VAT is not generally charged on non business transactions. For example, you would not have to charge VAT if you simply sold some of your spare DVDs to a friend.

1.2 Taxable persons

 Definition

Taxable persons are businesses which are (or should be) registered for VAT.

VAT registration rules are dealt with in Chapter 2.

A person can be an individual or a legal person such as a company.

1.3 Taxable supplies

Taxable supplies or outputs are most sales made by a taxable person. Taxable supplies can also include gifts and goods taken from the business for personal use.

1.4 Output tax

 Definition

The VAT charged on sales or taxable supplies is called **output tax.**

Taxable persons charge output tax to their customers and periodically, (usually quarterly), they pay it over to HM Revenue and Customs (HMRC).

1.5 Input tax

When a business buys goods or pays expenses (inputs), then it will also be paying VAT on those purchases or expenses.

 Definition

VAT paid by a business on purchases or expenses is called **input tax.**

Businesses are allowed to reclaim their input tax. They do this by deducting the input tax they have paid from the output tax which they owe, and paying over the net amount only. If the input tax exceeds the output tax, then the balance is recoverable from HMRC.

 Example

A business makes sales of £10,000 plus £1,750 of VAT. Its expenditure on purchases and expenses totals £7,000 plus £1,225 of VAT.

How much VAT is payable to HM Revenue and Customs?

Solution

	£
Output VAT	1,750.00
Less: Input VAT	(1,225.00)
VAT due	525.00

 Activity 1

Which of the following statements are correct?

1   VAT is a direct tax.
2   Jake is an AAT student working for a small accountancy practice. He advertises his bicycle for sale on the practice notice board and sells the bicycle to one of his workmates for £100. He should not charge VAT on the sale.
3   Businesses may keep all the VAT they collect from customers.

2 Types of supply

2.1 Classification of supplies

Supplies can be **taxable**, **exempt** or **outside the scope** of VAT.

VAT is charged on taxable supplies but not on exempt supplies or supplies outside the scope of VAT. It is therefore important to be able to correctly classify supplies in order to determine whether VAT should be charged.

Supplies outside the scope of VAT include items such as wages and dividends. They are ignored for VAT purposes and are not considered further.

2.2 Taxable supplies – rates of VAT

Taxable supplies are charged to VAT at one of three rates:

* **Zero rate:** This is a tax rate of nil. No VAT is charged but it is classed as a taxable supply. Therefore it is taken into account in deciding whether a trader should register for VAT and whether input VAT is recoverable.

* **Reduced rate:** Some supplies, mainly for domestic and charitable purposes are charged at the reduced rate. However, the reduced rate is not important for your assessment.

* **Standard rate:** Any taxable supply which is not charged at the zero or reduced rates is charged at the standard rate.

Currently the standard rate of VAT is 17.5%.

In order to calculate VAT on a VAT exclusive supply which is taxable at the standard rate, you multiply by 17.5%.

If the amount of the taxable supply is given as a VAT inclusive figure then you can find the amount of VAT included by multiplying by 17.5/117.5 (the VAT fraction). This is sometimes simplified to 7/47.

> ### Example
>
> A business makes taxable standard rated sales of £12,000.
>
> (i)   What is the VAT if this is a net of VAT amount?
> £12,000 × 17.5% = £2,100.00
>
> (ii) What is the VAT if this is a VAT inclusive amount?
> £12,000 × 17.5/117.5 = £1,787.23

If the rate of VAT were to increase to 20% then to calculate the VAT on a VAT exclusive supply you would multiply by 20%.

To find the VAT in an amount which included VAT at 20%, you would multiply by 20/120. (i.e. the VAT rate divided by 100 + the VAT rate).

2.3 Effect of making taxable supplies

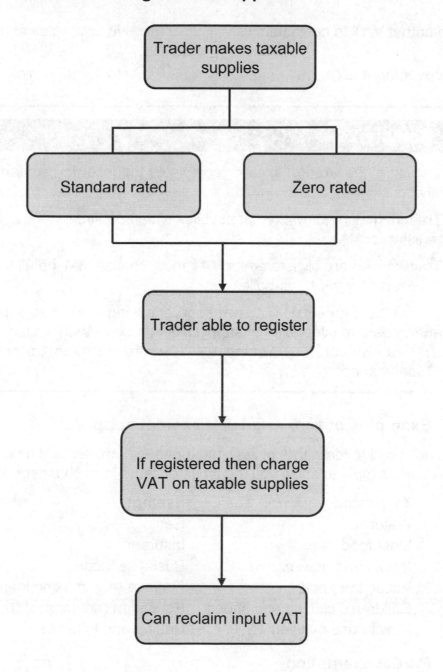

2.4 Differences between zero rated and exempt supplies

You must be careful to distinguish between traders making zero rated and exempt supplies.

	Exempt	Zero rated
Can register for VAT?	No	Yes
Charge output VAT to customers?	No	Yes at 0%
Can recover input tax?	No	Yes

 Activity 2

Select which of the word(s) in italics completes the following sentences correctly.

1 Traders making only exempt supplies …*can/must/cannot*…… register for VAT.

2 Traders who are registered for VAT must charge VAT on all their ….*taxable/exempt*… supplies.

3 One of the differences between traders making zero rated supplies and traders making exempt supplies is that zero rated traders …….*can/cannot*… recover input VAT, whereas exempt traders …..*can/cannot*.

2.5 Examples of zero rated and exempt supplies

You do not need to learn lists of zero rated and exempt items. These examples are simply to show you the types of items in each category.

Zero rated	Exempt
Water	Rent
Most food	Insurance
Books and newspapers	Postal services
Public transport	Finance (e.g. making loans)
Children's clothes and shoes	Education (not for profit)
New house building	Betting and lotteries

2.6 Partial exemption

A taxable person who makes both taxable supplies and exempt supplies is referred to as a **partially exempt** trader. For this purpose it does not matter if the taxable supplies are standard or zero rated.

The problem with partial exemption is that taxable supplies entitle the supplier to a credit for input tax, whereas exempt supplies do not. It is therefore necessary to apportion input tax between taxable and exempt supplies using a method set out by HMRC.

The most common method used is to divide input tax into three parts:

- Relating wholly to taxable supplies – all recoverable

- Relating wholly to exempt supplies – irrecoverable (but see below)

- Relating to overheads – proportion which relate to taxable supplies can be recovered, leaving the rest irrecoverable (but see below)

If the total irrecoverable input tax is less than a certain amount, the **de minimis limit**, then it **can** be recovered. If irrecoverable input tax is less than:

- £625 per month on average and

- less than 50% of total input tax

then it can be recovered.

 Example

Jason runs a business which makes both taxable and exempt supplies. He is preparing his VAT return for the quarter ended 31 March 20X1.

His total input tax for the quarter is £4,560 of which £1,740 is attributable to exempt supplies.

How much input tax can he reclaim for the quarter?

Solution

He can reclaim £4,560.

The input tax attributable to exempt supplies, which is normally irrecoverable, is £580 per month (£1,740/3). This is less than £625 per month on average and the total exempt input tax is less than 50% of the total input tax.

Note that for assessment purposes, you need an awareness of the basics of this topic but calculations of the amount of exempt input tax will not be required.

3 Recovery of input tax

3.1 Conditions

Input VAT is recoverable by registered traders on goods and services which are supplied to them for business purposes. A VAT invoice (see Chapter 3) is usually needed to support the claim.

3.2 Irrecoverable (blocked) input VAT

Input VAT on the following goods and services cannot be recovered:

- Business entertaining, although VAT incurred on staff entertaining is recoverable

- Purchase of cars, unless they are 100% used for business purposes (e.g. car owned by a driving school purely used to give driving lessons).

3.3 Motor expenses

A business can recover input VAT incurred on the running costs of a car such as fuel and repairs, even when there is some private use of the car.

When a business pays fuel costs for an employee or sole trader, and there is some private use of the vehicle, extra output tax will be payable. This extra output tax is called a **fuel scale charge** and varies with the CO_2 emissions of the car. The fuel scale charge is a **VAT inclusive figure** so the VAT element is calculated as 7/47.

Note that the scale charges are given in 5 g/km intervals. If a car has an emission figure which is not exactly equal to one of the scale charges on the list, then it has to be rounded down to the next lower figure.

 Example

Forge Ltd provides a company car to Charles and pays for all his private fuel. The CO_2 emission level of the car is 204 g/km.

The scale charge table shows (for a 3 month period):

200 g/km	£350 (net)	VAT £61.25
205 g/km	£362 (net)	VAT £63.35

£350 will be added to the total outputs on the company's VAT return and additional output tax of £61.25 will be payable by the company.

Note that for assessment purposes, you need to be aware of the fuel scale charges and the effect on the total VAT payable / reclaimable, but that calculations will not be required.

4 Output tax

4.1 Introduction

Registered traders must charge output tax on all taxable supplies at the appropriate rate. This includes sales of capital assets.

4.2 Sales of capital assets

Normally when a trader sells a capital asset they will charge VAT at the standard rate on the sale price. However if the asset is a car on which the input tax was blocked (i.e. the trader could not recover the input tax), then no output VAT is charged as it is an exempt sale. If the input VAT was recoverable on the car, then output VAT is charged on the sale price as normal.

 Activity 3

You are given the following information about sales of capital assets in the quarter to 31.12.X1.

Complete the table to show the amount of output tax that must be charged on each item.

Item	Input tax recovered	Sale proceeds (excl VAT) £	Output tax £
Van	Yes	11,000	
Car (1)	Yes	9,500	
Car (2)	No	10,550	
Machinery	Yes	21,000	

4.3 Goods for own use

When a sole trader or partner in a partnership takes goods out of the business for their own use, an accounting adjustment should be made to charge the goods to the trader's drawings account.

Output VAT must also be charged on the replacement cost of goods taken.

This output VAT must be paid by the business and debited to the drawings account. The credit entry will be made in the VAT account.

 Example

Beverley is a registered trader. In the quarter to 30.9.X1 she takes goods worth £500 from stock for her own use and withdraws £6,000 in cash.

How much output VAT should be accounted for on these drawings?

Solution

Output VAT of £87.50 (£500 × 17.5%) is due on the drawings of goods.

No output VAT is charged on cash drawings.

5 Sources of information

5.1 Legislation

The main source of law on VAT is the VAT Act 1994 as amended by annual Finance Acts and other regulations issued by Parliament.

5.2 HMRC website

HMRC expect taxpayers to be able to answer many of their queries by searching the HMRC website at http://www.hmrc.gov.uk. Many of the HMRC publications are available to download and there a number of frequently asked questions to review.

5.3 VAT guide

HMRC issue a booklet called the **VAT Guide** Notice 700. This is the main guide to VAT rules and procedures. There are a number of supplements and amendments to the Guide to keep it up to date.

The VAT Guide is also available online on the HMRC website. As it is a large document (over 250 pages long) it is broken into sections on the website. It can be searched online or downloaded.

If you are dealing with accounting for VAT and VAT returns in practice, then you should become familiar with the contents of the VAT Guide in order to be able to refer to it when necessary.

 Example

If you wished to look up more information about the topics covered so far in this chapter, then Section 3 of the VAT guide has the following contents.

3. General explanation of VAT: introduction and liability

3.1 Introduction to VAT

3.2 What is VAT about?

3.3 How many rates of VAT are there?

3.4 What supplies are reduced-rated?

3.5 Is VAT payable on zero-rated supplies?

3.6 Is VAT payable on exempt supplies?

3.7 Where can I find further information on liability and rates of tax?

5.4 VAT Notes

HMRC also publish a quarterly bulletin called VAT Notes. This is sent to all registered traders and contains a summary of all recent changes to the VAT rules and announces future changes.

5.5 VAT helpline

If a taxpayer cannot find the answer to their queries on the HMRC website then a telephone helpline is available.

Taxpayers can also email or write to HMRC with VAT queries.

 6 HM Revenue and Customs

6.1 Introduction

As mentioned above, **HM Revenue and Customs** (HMRC) is the government body that is responsible for administering VAT.

VAT offices across the country are responsible for the local administration of VAT within a particular geographical area. Local VAT offices deal with the collection of outstanding tax and carry out visits to taxpayers to check that they are complying with VAT rules.

HMRC are also responsible for dealing with all other issues concerning VAT including registration and record keeping (see below for record keeping requirements).

6.2   HMRC powers

HMRC have certain powers that help it administer the tax. These include:

- Inspecting premises
- Examining records
- Making assessments for underpaid tax
- Charging penalties for breaches of VAT rules (more detail on penalties can be found in Chapter 5)
- Determining whether certain supplies are liable for VAT.

6.3   HMRC rulings

HMRC will give rulings on how they will deal with particular transactions. This ruling is binding on HMRC provided the taxpayer has given all the necessary facts. However, it is not binding on the taxpayer who may choose to ignore the ruling, although this will almost certainly lead to a dispute with HMRC that will need to be resolved by the Tax Tribunal.

Obtaining a ruling on areas of difficulty is recommended by HMRC. This is the advice they give on their website.

"We recognise the importance for taxpayers and their advisers of being able to acquire timely and accurate advice and rulings about VAT.

Most enquiries can be dealt with by phoning our advice service. But for your own protection, you should put any major issues and more detailed questions in writing."

6.4   Communicating with HMRC

In your assessment you may be asked to draft or complete a brief letter to HMRC to ask for information or guidance.

The letter should give the name, address, telephone number and VAT registration number of the business. You may not have to complete all these details. You should set out the nature of the query or information required.

Example

You are Jan Smith, an AAT student who works in the accounts department of Dorn Ltd, which is a VAT registered company. The company's VAT registration number is 1R3 45678. Its address is 14 Camberwell Road, Surbiton and its telephone number is 080 456 1234.

The company manufactures widgets which it sells to large retail stores. The company has just started to sell the widgets via mail order and you have been asked to find out how any postal charges (1% of VAT exclusive cost with a minimum charge of £2.50) should be dealt with for VAT purposes.

A suggested letter would be as follows.

> Dorn Ltd
> 14 Camberwell Road
> Surbiton
> Tel: 080 456 1234
> 14 May 20X1

VAT registration number: 1R3 45678

To: HMRC
Local office address

Dear Sir/Madam

Treatment of postal charges for VAT mail order for Dorn Ltd

I have a query concerning postal charges on mail order sales for Dorn Ltd.

Dorn Ltd currently manufactures widgets and sells them to retail stores. This is a standard rated business.

Mail order sales within the UK have recently started and a separate postal charge is levied. This is 1% of the cost of widgets sold (excluding VAT), subject to a minimum charge of £2.50.

The query concerns the postal charges. I would be grateful if you could say how these should be treated for VAT.

I look forward to your reply.

Kind regards

Jan Smith

In your assessment you will only be asked to complete a short piece of communication.

Note that in practice, HMRC expect you to check the information publicly available in the VAT Guide 700 and on their website before submitting a query.

6.5 Disputes with HMRC

Most disagreements between the taxpayer and HMRC are resolved quickly, but if an agreement cannot be reached then the taxpayer has a choice of actions.

(1) Ask for their case to be reviewed by another HMRC officer who has not previously been involved with the matter.

(2) If they do not wish the case to be reviewed by another officer, or if they disagree with the review findings, then the taxpayer can appeal to the Tax Tribunal. Such appeals are made initially to the First-tier Tax Tribunal. If the matter cannot be resolved there it may be appealed upwards to the Upper Tribunal and from there to the Court of Appeal and then the Supreme Court.

The ultimate legal authority on VAT matters is the European Court of Justice.

7 Test your knowledge

 Test your knowledge

Having completed Chapter 1 you should now be able to attempt:

Practice Activities 1 to 10

8   Summary

In this introductory chapter we looked at some of the basic principles and terminology used when dealing with VAT.

You should now understand that VAT is an indirect tax borne by the final consumer but collected on behalf of the government by businesses.

An important area covered in this chapter is the distinction between taxable and exempt supplies. Businesses making only exempt supplies cannot register for VAT or reclaim input tax. Some input tax cannot be recovered by a business.

If you need to find out more about VAT then it is important to know where to look. The VAT guide 700 and the HMRC website cover everything a typical business would need to know about VAT. Of course, you do not need to know all this material, simply to know where you might look to find it.

Communicating with HMRC is an important element of the exam. You must understand the importance of getting rulings on contentious matters in writing.

Answers to chapter activities

Activity 1

1   VAT is an indirect tax so the statement is incorrect.

2   VAT is charged on business transactions so the statement is correct. Jake does not need to charge VAT on the sale of his bicycle.

3   Businesses collect VAT on behalf of the government so this statement is incorrect.

Activity 2

1   Cannot.

2   Taxable.

3   Can
    Cannot.

Activity 3

Van	£1,925.00
Car 1	£1,662.50
Car 2	Nil – exempt
Machinery	£3,675.00

VAT registration

2

Introduction

This chapter introduces the rules for both compulsory and voluntary VAT registration. It also explains when a business must deregister.

If a business does not register for VAT when it starts then a careful eye must be kept on the level of taxable turnover, (standard and zero rated supplies), to avoid missing the deadline for registration.

Remember from Chapter 1 that a taxable person is one who is, or should be, registered for VAT. This means that even if a trader does not register, they may still have a liability for VAT and they may be charged a penalty.

KNOWLEDGE	CONTENTS
Explain the VAT registration requirements (1.3)	1 Compulsory registration 2 Consequences of registration 3 Voluntary registration 4 Deregistration 5 Record keeping

1 Compulsory registration

1.1 Introduction

Not all businesses need to register for VAT even if they make taxable supplies. It is only businesses that have taxable supplies exceeding the registration limits that have to register under the compulsory registration rules.

There are two separate tests for compulsory registration:

* Historic test

* Future prospects test

Note that taxable supplies for registration purposes are made up of all taxable supplies (standard, reduced and zero rated) excluding VAT and excluding the sales of capital assets. The level of exempt supplies made is not relevant in deciding whether a business has to register.

1.2 Historic test

At the end of each month, the trader must look at the cumulative total of taxable supplies for the last 12 months (or since starting in business if this is less than 12 months ago).

If the total exceeds the registration limit then the trader must register as follows:

* Notify HMRC **within 30 days** of the end of the month in which the turnover limit is exceeded. Notification can be made online or by post.

* Registration is effective from the **end of the month** following the month in which turnover exceeded the limit, or an agreed earlier date.

* A trader need not register if his taxable supplies for the next 12 months are expected to be less than the deregistration limit (see below). This helps businesses whose annual turnover is usually below the registration limit but which have experienced one particularly good year.

Note that you are not expected to memorise the current registration limits. You would be given this information in an exam if needed.

Example

Tariq started in business on 1 February 20X0.

He checks his taxable turnover at the end of each month and discovers at the end of July 20X1 that his taxable supplies for the previous 12 months have exceeded the registration limit.

He must notify HMRC by 30 August and will be registered with effect from 1 September 20X1 or an agreed earlier date.

 Activity 1

Deanna starts a business on 1 June 20X0.

Her monthly turnover of taxable supplies is £7,000.

1   Assuming the registration limit is £68,000, when does Deanna have to notify HMRC of her liability to register and from which date would she normally be registered?

2   Would your answer to (a) be any different if Deanna's turnover was made up of half standard rated and half zero rated supplies?

3   Would your answer to (a) be any different if Deanna's turnover was made up wholly of exempt supplies?

1.3   Future prospects test

A liability to register will also arise if taxable supplies within the next 30 days are expected to exceed the registration limit. This test is applied at any time, not just the end of a month, and only looks at the supplies to be made in the next 30 days in isolation.

- HMRC must be notified **before the end** of the 30 day period.

- Registration will be effective from the **beginning** of the 30 day period.

Example

Dog Ltd signs a lease for new business premises on 1 June 20X0 and opens for business on 15 September 20X0. The company estimates that taxable supplies will be £75,000 per month starting immediately.

Assuming the registration limit is £68,000, when does Dog Ltd have to register for VAT and notify HMRC?

Solution

Dog Ltd is liable to registration because supplies for the 30 days to 14 October 20X0 are expected to exceed £68,000.

The company must notify HMRC of its liability to registration by 14 October 20X0 and is registered with effect from 15 September 20X0.

Note: Dog Ltd does not make any taxable supplies before September 20X0 so does not need to register before that date.

 Activity 2

State which of the following unregistered traders are liable to register for VAT and the effective date of registration.

Assume the registration limit is £68,000.

Name	Supplies	Details
Majid	Accountancy services	Started in business on 1 October 20X0 with estimated fees of £15,000 per month.
Jane	Baby wear	Established the business on 1 July 20X0 when Jane signed a contract to supply a local nursery. Sales for July 20X0 are expected to be £90,000.
Sayso Ltd	Insurance broker	Commenced trading 2 August 20X0 with expected sales of £100,000 per month. Insurance broking is an exempt activity.

1.4 Number of registrations

A person can be registered only once, and this registration includes all the businesses that person carries on.

Where a partnership is concerned, separate businesses carried on by the same partners will have a single registration.

Companies are all registered individually although it is possible for companies in certain sorts of groups to have a single registration. You do not need to know any details of this.

 Example

Jason is a sole trader. He owns a clothing shop "Jason's Style" which is open during the day, and in the evenings he runs a business organising parties. Both businesses have turnover of £40,000 each.

Jason is also a partner in Bash and Co, an import/export business he helps run with his wife. The partnership business has a turnover of £100,000.

Jason is also a shareholder in Xenon Ltd, a company specialising in manufacturing electronic equipment. The company has a turnover of £250,000.

Assuming the entire business turnover is of taxable supplies in each case, how many VAT registrations are required to cover these businesses? Assume the registration limit is £68,000.

Solution

There are three registrations needed here:

(a)   One registration is needed to cover Jason's two sole trader businesses. Even though each business has turnover below the registration limit, the combined turnover of the businesses is over the limit.

(b)   One registration will cover Bash and Co.

(c)   The third registration will be needed to cover Xenon Ltd.

1.5 Exemption from registration

A trader making only zero rated supplies can apply for exemption from registration. However, this would mean they cannot recover their input tax, and so is only likely if the trader does not want the administrative burden of complying with VAT regulations.

2 Consequences of registration

2.1 Accounting for VAT

Once registered, a taxable person must start accounting for VAT.

- Output tax must be charged on taxable supplies.

- Each registered trader is allocated a VAT registration number, which must be quoted on all invoices.

- Each registered trader is allocated a tax period for filing returns, which is normally every three months.

- Input tax on most business purchases and expenses can be recovered. (Some exceptions were seen in Chapter 1.) This can also include certain input VAT incurred before registration.

- Appropriate VAT records must be kept (see section 5 below).

Traders will be sent a certificate of registration which contains their registration number and is their proof of registration.

2.2 Failure to register

A trader might think they could avoid VAT by not registering. However, if a trader does not register when they go over the compulsory registration limit then there are two consequences.

(i) All the VAT that the trader **should have charged** from the date they **should have registered** is payable to HMRC. As the trader cannot now go back to their customers and charge them the VAT, they will have to pay over the VAT out of their own profits.

(ii) A penalty can be charged. This is a percentage of the VAT due.

 Example

Beverley runs a business manufacturing silicon cookware which is a standard rated supply. She has failed to register for VAT.

On 1 October 20X0 she discovers she should have been registered since 1 March 20X0. Her turnover since that date is £25,000.

Beverley will have to pay over VAT of £3,723.40 (17.5/117.5 × £25,000) less any input tax she has suffered in this period.

3 Voluntary registration

3.1 Actual or intending traders

Even if they are not required to register, a person can register provided they are **making or intending to make taxable supplies**.

HMRC will register the trader from the date of the request for voluntary registration, or a mutually agreed earlier date.

Remember that a trader who only makes exempt supplies cannot register.

3.2 Advantages and disadvantages of voluntary registration

Advantages	Disadvantages
Avoids penalties for late registration.	Business will have to comply with the VAT administration rules which may take time away from running the business.
Can recover input VAT on purchases and expenses.	Business must charge VAT. This makes their goods more expensive than an unregistered trader selling the same items or services. This extra cost cannot be recovered by unregistered customers such as the general public.
Can disguise the small size of the business.	

4 Deregistration

4.1 Compulsory deregistration

A person must deregister when he ceases to make taxable supplies.

- HMRC should be notified within 30 days of ceasing to make taxable supplies.

- VAT registration is cancelled from the date of cessation or a mutually agreed later date.

4.2 Voluntary deregistration

A person may voluntarily deregister, even if the business continues, if there is evidence that taxable supplies in the next 12 months will not exceed the deregistration limit. The deregistration limit is always slightly lower than the registration limit.

- The 12 month period can start at any time. It does not have to be the beginning or end of a month.

- The trader must prove to HMRC that they qualify.

- VAT registration is cancelled from the date of the request or an agreed later date.

4.3 Effect of deregistration

On deregistration, VAT output tax must be paid over on the value of capital assets and stock owned at the date of deregistration. This takes back the input tax relief that the business would have had when it bought those assets or stock.

 Activity 3

Jig Ltd closes down its business on 10 October 20X0.

At 1 May 20X0, Eli thinks that his taxable turnover for the year to 30 April 20X1 will be below the deregistration limit. He immediately applies for deregistration.

State when Jig Ltd should notify HMRC of the business cessation and from when the business will be deregistered.

State when Eli will be deregistered.

5 Record keeping

5.1 General requirements

Businesses must keep information which will allow HMRC to check VAT returns adequately. Generally, the business must keep records of:

- all taxable and exempt supplies made in the course of business

- all taxable supplies received in the course of business

- a summary of the total output tax and input tax for each tax period – the VAT account (see Chapter 6).

Failure to keep records can lead to a penalty.

5.2 Details to be kept

The business must keep records to prove the figures shown on the VAT returns for the previous six years, although HMRC can reduce this period where the records are bulky and the information they contain can be provided in another way. These records might include the following:

- orders and delivery notes

- relevant business correspondence

- appointment and job books

- purchases and sales books

- cash books and other account books

- bank statements, paying-in slips and cheque stubs

- purchase invoices and copy sales invoices

- recordings of daily takings, including till rolls

- annual accounts

- import and export documents

- VAT accounts

- any credit notes issued or received.

Registered businesses may be visited by a VAT officer on occasion to ensure that their records are being correctly maintained.

5.3 Electronic and paper VAT records

As long as the VAT records meet the requirements laid down by HMRC, they can be kept in whatever format – paper and/or electronic – that the business prefers.

Where a business keeps all or part of its records on a computer, it must make sure that the records are easily accessible if a VAT officer visits.

Records can be kept on microfilm provided HMRC have given approval and the records can be inspected when necessary.

Some businesses send or receive invoices by electronic means. This does not require approval from HMRC.

You should be able to list the records that must be kept for VAT purposes.

6 Test your knowledge

 Test your knowledge

Having completed Chapter 2 you should now be able to attempt:

Practice Activities 11 to 16.

7 Summary

In this chapter we have considered which traders need to become VAT registered and the effects of registration.

Both the historic and future prospects test for registration have been set out. Remember that it is the turnover of taxable supplies, including zero-rated supplies, that determines whether a business needs to register for VAT.

It is also important to remember that businesses which **only** make **exempt** supplies **cannot** register for VAT whilst businesses that **only** make **zero-rated** supplies **need not** register for VAT if they do not wish.

Failure to register when taxable supplies have exceeded the limit can cost a business a great deal. Firstly they must pay over the VAT they should have collected from customers and secondly they may be charged a penalty.

Traders can also choose to register voluntarily provided they are making taxable supplies now or intend to in the future. This allows the business to recover input tax, but may make the price of their goods comparatively more expensive than those of an unregistered trader

We saw that a business **must** deregister if it ceases to make taxable supplies, and **may** deregister if its taxable supplies for the next 12 months will be below the deregistration limit.

Finally the records that must be kept by a registered business were discussed.

Answers to chapter activities

Activity 1

1   Deanna's taxable turnover will exceed £68,000 after 10 months which is at the end of March 20X1. She must notify HMRC by 30 April 20X1 and will be registered with effect from 1 May 20X1.

2   No – taxable supplies includes both standard rated and zero rated supplies.

3   Yes – traders who only make exempt supplies cannot register.

Activity 2

Majid will exceed the registration threshold after 5 months in business, that is at the end of February 20X1. He must notify HMRC by 30 March and will be registered from 1 April.

Jane must register under the future prospects test as her sales will immediately exceed the registration limit within the next 30 days. She must notify HMRC by 30 July and will be registered from 1 July.

Sayso Ltd cannot register as they only make exempt supplies.

Activity 3

Jig Ltd must notify HMRC of their business cessation by 9 November 20X0. The business will be deregistered from 10 October 20X0 or a mutually agreed later date.

Eli's registration will be cancelled with effect from 1 May 20X0 or an agreed later date.

VAT documentation

Introduction

This chapter looks at how VAT is collected via a VAT invoice and all the details that are required to be shown on such an invoice. Other documents such as credit notes and proforma invoices are also covered.

The rules for tax points are also covered. A tax point is the date which determines in which VAT period the VAT on transactions should be included.

Finally, the importance of keeping staff up to date on changes in VAT legislation is discussed.

KNOWLEDGE
Identify the information that must be included on business documentation of VAT- registered businesses (1.4)
Recognise different types of inputs and outputs (1.5)

SKILLS
Calculate accurately relevant inputs and outputs (1.2)
Advise relevant people of the impact that any changes in VAT legislation, including the VAT rate, would have on the organisation's recording systems (2.2)

CONTENTS
1   VAT invoices
2   Tax points
3   Other documentation
4   Changes in VAT legislation

1 VAT invoices

1.1 Introduction

All businesses that are registered for VAT must provide evidence to VAT registered customers of the VAT they have been charged. In order to do this the supplier must give or send to the purchaser a VAT invoice **within 30 days** of the earlier of:

- supply of the goods or services or
- receipt of the payment.

VAT invoices are not required:

- if the purchaser is not VAT registered or
- if the supply is wholly zero rated.

In practice it is impossible to tell if a purchaser is VAT registered or not, so traders normally issue a VAT invoice anyway. If they are retailers selling to the public they have special rules (see below). Similarly, traders will normally issue invoices for zero rated sales which show the same details as for other supplies, but technically this is not a VAT invoice.

The original VAT invoice is sent to the customer and forms their evidence for reclaiming input VAT. A copy must be kept by the supplier to support the calculation of output VAT.

1.2 Form of a VAT invoice

There is **no standard format for invoices**. The exact design is the choice of the business, but it must show the following details (unless the invoice is a **less detailed tax invoice** that you will see later):

- identifying number which must follow a sequence
- date of supply (or tax point – see below) and the date of issue of the invoice
- supplier's name and address and registration number
- name and address of customer, i.e. the person to whom the goods or services are supplied
- type of supply
    - sale
    - hire purchase, credit sale, conditional sale or similar transaction
    - loan

- – exchange
- – hire, lease or rental
- – process (making goods using the customer's own materials)
- – sale on commission (e.g. an estate agent)
- – supply on sale or return
- description of the goods or services
- quantity of goods or extent of services
- rate of tax and amount payable (in sterling) excluding VAT for each separate description
- total amount payable (excluding VAT) in sterling
- rate of any cash discount offered (these are also called settlement discounts)
- separate rate and amount of VAT charged for each rate of VAT
- total amount of VAT chargeable.

1.3 VAT and discounts

If a **trade discount** is given then this is deducted before VAT is calculated.

If a **settlement discount** is offered, then the VAT is always calculated as if the customer takes the maximum discount.

 Example

Joachim is in business manufacturing angle brackets which he sells to retailers. He offers a 5% discount if goods are paid for within 10 days and a 2% discount if goods are paid for within 21 days.

He sells angle brackets with a pre-discount price of £1,000 to Kim Ltd.

How much VAT should he charge on the invoice assuming that the rate of VAT is 17.5%?

Solution

VAT should be calculated on the lowest amount a customer could pay. This is £166.25 (£1,000 × 95% × 17.5%)

1.4 Example of a VAT invoice

💡 Example

MICRO TRAINING GROUP LTD
Unit 34
Castlewell Trading Estate
Manchester
M12 5RHF

To:

Slough Labels Ltd	Sales invoice number:	35
Station Unit	VAT registration number:	234 5566 87
Slough	Date of issue:	30 September 20X0
SL1 3EJ	Tax point:	12 September 20X0

Sales:

Quantity	Description and price	Amount ex VAT	VAT rate	VAT
6	Programmable calculators			
	FR34 at £24.76	148.56	17.5%	
12	Programmable calculators			
	GT60 at £36.80	441.60	17.5%	
		590.16		101.21
	Delivery	23.45	17.5%	4.02
		613.61		105.23
VAT		105.23		
TOTAL		718.84		

Terms: Net 30 days. Cash discount of 2% if paid within 10 days

On this invoice the VAT is calculated after applying the discount of 2%.

Activity 1

An invoice is issued for standard rated goods with a list price of £380.00 (excluding VAT). A 10% trade discount is given and a 4% settlement or cash discount is offered.

How much VAT should be included on the invoice?

1.5 Rounding VAT

Usually, the amount of VAT calculated will not be a whole number of pounds and pence. You will therefore need a rounding adjustment. The rules governing this adjustment are quite tricky, and permit more than one method. However, for assessment purposes you only need to know the basic rounding rule – that is that the total amount of VAT payable on an invoice can be rounded down to the nearest penny.

 Activity 2

Given below are the totals from three VAT invoices

Invoice	Description and price	Net of VAT	VAT rate	VAT
1	16 × 6 metre hosepipes @£3.23 each	51.68	17.5%	
2	24 × bags of compost @ £5.78 each	138.72	17.5%	
3	Supply of kitchen units	1,084.50	17.5%	

Calculate the total VAT to be charged in each case.

1.6 Less detailed VAT invoices

Retailers (selling to the public), do not have to issue a detailed VAT invoice every time they make a sale as this would make trading in a busy shop impossible.

If the total amount of the supply (including VAT) by the retailer does not exceed £250, then **when a customer requests a tax invoice** a retailer may issue a **less detailed tax invoice**. However, if requested by a customer a full VAT invoice must be issued.

The details required on the invoice are:

- supplier's name and address

- supplier's VAT registration number

- date of supply

- description sufficient to identify the goods or services

- amount payable (including VAT) for each rate (standard and zero)

- the VAT rate applicable

The main differences here are that the customer's name and address can be omitted, and the total on the invoice includes the VAT without the VAT itself being shown separately.

Although this invoice shows less detail, it is still a valid tax invoice. This means that if the purchaser is a VAT registered business they can use the invoice to support a claim for input VAT.

Retailers do not have to keep copies of the less detailed VAT invoices that they issue, whereas non retailers must keep copies of all sales invoices issued. This is because retailers generally calculate their VAT from their **daily gross takings** rather than from individual invoices.

 Example

Delta Office Supplies

46, Central Mall, Glastonbury, Somerset
G34 7QT
Telephone: 01392 43215

15 April 20X0

1 box of 50 blank DVD-R
Total including VAT @ 17.5%   £25.85

VAT registration number: 653 7612 44

1.7   Modified invoices

If a trader sell goods or a service for more than £250 including VAT, and the customer agrees, they may issue a modified VAT invoice. This shows the VAT inclusive amount for each item sold and then at the bottom of the invoice the following amounts must be shown:

- the overall VAT inclusive total

- the total amount of VAT included in the total

- the total value of the supplies net of VAT

- the total value of any zero-rated and exempt supplies

This only saves the trader from including the individual cost net of VAT and the VAT rate for each item. All other details must be the same as for a full VAT invoice.

2 Tax points

2.1 Introduction

 Definition

The **tax point** is the date on which the liability for output tax arises – it is the date on which a supply is recorded as taking place for the purposes of the tax return.

Most taxable persons make a VAT return each quarter. The return must include all supplies whose tax points fall within that quarter.

2.2 The basic tax point

The **basic tax point** for goods is the date of delivery of those goods or the date the customer takes the goods away. For services, the tax point is the date the services are performed.

 Example

Queue Ltd received an order for goods from a customer on 14 March. The goods were despatched on 18 March and the customer paid on 15 April when they received their invoice dated 13 April.

State the basic tax point date.

Solution

The tax point is 18 March, i.e. the date of despatch.

2.3　Actual tax point

The basic tax point is amended in two situations.

Earlier tax point	Later tax point
• A tax invoice is issued or a payment is received before the basic tax point	• A tax invoice is issued within 14 days after the basic tax point (14 day rule)
• In these circumstances the date of invoice or payment is the time when the supply is treated as taking place.	• In these circumstances the date of issue of the invoice is the time when the supply is treated as taking place

Provided that written approval is received from the local VAT office, the 14 day rule can be varied, for example to accommodate a supplier who issues all of his invoices each month on the last day of the month.

The 14 day rule cannot apply to invoices for zero rated goods as these are not tax invoices. Most exports are zero rated (see Chapter 6 for more details), so the tax point for these goods is always the earlier of the supply of goods and the receipt of payment.

2.4　Deposits received in advance

If a business receives a deposit or part payment in advance then this creates a tax point when the deposit is received. However, this is only for the deposit, not the whole supply. The business must acount for the VAT included in the deposit.

No tax point is created for a returnable deposit, e.g. a deposit required to ensure the safe return of a hired item, where the deposit is returned to the customer when they bring the item back safely.

KAPLAN PUBLISHING

Example

Ahmed receives a £50 deposit from a customer on 1 July. The total cost of the item is £200 including VAT at 17.5% and the customer pays the balance of £150 on 12 September when they collect the goods.

How is VAT accounted for on this transaction?

Solution

The deposit of £50 creates a tax point on 1 July.
The amount of VAT is £7.44 (£50 × 17.5/117.5) and this must be entered in the VAT return which includes 1 July.

The payment on 12 September creates a further tax point.
The VAT is £22.34 (£150 × 17.5/117.5) and this must be included in the VAT return which includes 12 September.

Activity 3

In each of the following cases state the tax point date.

1   Goods delivered to a customer on 10 July, invoice sent out on 15 July and payment received 30 July.
2   Invoice sent out to a customer on 12 August, goods delivered to the customer on 16 August, payment received 20 September.
3   Payment received from customer on 4 September, goods sent to customer on 5 September with an invoice dated on that day.
4   Goods delivered to a customer on 13 September, invoice sent out on 30 September and payment received 31 October.

3   Other documentation

3.1   Credit notes and VAT

When customers return goods which were taxable supplies, the supplier may issue a credit note. This has to have similar information to that found on the original invoice and must be **clearly labelled as a credit note**. It should contain:

- an identifying number and date of issue
- the supplier's name, address and registration number

- the customer's name and address

- the reason for the credit (e.g. goods returned)

- a description of the goods or services for which the credit is being allowed

- the quantity and amount credited for each description

- the total amount credited, excluding VAT

- the rate and amount credited

The number and date of the original tax invoice should also appear on the credit note.

If the supplier issues the credit note without making a VAT adjustment, the credit note must say '**This is not a credit note for VAT'.**

A supplier is not allowed to issue a credit note to recover VAT on bad debts.

3.2   Proforma invoices

When a business issues a sales invoice that includes VAT, the VAT becomes payable to HMRC next time the business submits a return.

This can cause cashflow problems if the customer has not yet paid the invoice, because the business then has to pay over the VAT before collecting it from their customers.

To avoid this, a business may issue a **proforma invoice** which essentially is a demand for payment. Once payment is received, the business will then issue a 'live' invoice to replace the proforma.

Because a proforma invoice does not rank as a VAT invoice the supplier is not required to pay VAT to HMRC until the 'live' invoice is issued. For this reason, the customer cannot reclaim VAT on a proforma invoice but must instead wait until the valid VAT invoice is received.

Proforma invoices must be clearly marked with the words '**This is not a VAT invoice'.**

3.3   Statements and demands for payment

It is important to appreciate that only VAT invoices and credit notes should be entered in the VAT records. When a business sends out a demand for payment or a statement there is no VAT implication. VAT has already been recorded and the demand or statement is simply the business trying to collect what it is owed.

3.4 Orders and delivery notes

These are also ignored for VAT and cannot be used by a customer as evidence for reclaiming VAT on their purchases.

3.5 VAT only invoices

Sometimes a business needs to increase VAT charged on an earlier invoice or may have forgotten to include VAT. One solution would be to credit the original invoice and then reinvoice it. Alternatively the business can issue an invoice just for the VAT and label it as a VAT only invoice.

Such an invoice must be entered in the VAT records and the tax paid over to HMRC as usual. A registered purchaser who receives the invoice will treat it as a normal VAT invoice and be able to recover the VAT charged.

4 Changes in VAT legislation

4.1 Change in the rate of VAT

The tax point date becomes very important when there is a change in the rate of VAT or if a supply is reclassified from one rate of VAT to another.

For example, during 2009 the standard rate of VAT was temporarily reduced to 15%, reverting back to 17.5% on 1 January 2010. A net supply of £100 made on 31 December would have VAT of £15.00 and on 1 January 2010 £17.50.

In the assessment you may be required to calculate VAT from net sales amounts at different rates of VAT from the current rate of 17.5%, including cases where settlement discounts are offered.

4.2 Effect of a VAT rate change on a business

A change in the rate of VAT has a major effect on the business accounting system including the following:

- Sales invoices need to be produced with the correct rate of VAT.

- Sales prices used in quotes or for pricing invoices must include the correct rate of VAT.

- Retail businesses need to make sure that prices displayed to the public are correct.

- Staff expense claims must reclaim the correct rate of VAT on (for example) mileage expenses.

- The correct input tax reclaim must be made for purchases and expenses. Input VAT claimed should be whatever figure is shown on the invoice for the purchase or expense. However, staff would need to know the details of any rate change so that they can query any actual errors with suppliers.

However, whether or not a change in VAT rate is passed on to the customer is a commercial decision for a business to make. The current prices can be maintained and the cost of a VAT increase (or profit from a VAT decrease) can be absorbed by the business.

In a manual system it is important that all relevant staff are notified of the change and its impact and that price lists are updated.

In a computerised system the accounting software must be updated to produce sales invoices at the correct rate and to deal with differing rates of VAT on purchase invoices. If the VAT is calculated at the point of sale by the till system, the system must be adjusted to take account of the new rate.

In both cases it is important that the change takes place at the correct time. For example, new prices would need to be quoted to customers from the date of change. However, sales invoices must use the rate of VAT relevant to the tax point date and not necessarily the date the invoice is raised.

4.3   Informing staff

A number of different staff within a business would need to be told about a rate change and its effects.

- IT department staff – to ensure the relevant changes are made to the computerised accounting system.

- Sales ledger staff – to raise or check sales invoices correctly.

- Purchase ledger staff – so that they can check purchase invoices correctly.

- Sales staff – to ensure customers are given correct prices.

- Marketing department staff – so that any new brochures or publicity material is correct.

- Staff generally – to ensure their expense claims are made correctly.

In your assessment you may have to draft or complete a simple email advising relevant people of the change.

Example

To: Sales ledger staff

From: Junior Accountant

Subject: Change in the rate of VAT

Date: 14/3/20X0

Please note that the standard rate of VAT which applies to all our products will change on 1 April 20X0 from 17.5% to 20%.

Any invoices with a tax point of 1 April or later must have the new VAT rate applied.

It is important that invoices with a tax point before 1 April continue to include VAT at the old rate.

5 Test your knowledge

 Test your knowledge

Having completed Chapter 3 you should now be able to attempt:

Practice Activities 17 to 23

6 Summary

This chapter has covered two important areas for VAT – invoicing and tax points.

VAT invoices must include certain details and in normal circumstances must be given or sent to a VAT registered purchaser. In practice this means that all purchasers will be provided with a VAT invoice whether they are registered or not. However retailers are allowed to issue less detailed or modified invoices. Credit notes sent out by a business must include the same details as the invoice.

Proforma invoices must not include VAT.

The tax point for a supply of goods is important as this determines the VAT period in which the VAT on those goods is included. The basic tax point is the date on which goods are delivered or collected by a customer but there are also situations in which the tax point can be earlier or later. These rules must be learned.

Changes in the rate of VAT have a major impact on a business' recording system and you should have a basic understanding of this,

Answers to chapter activities

Activity 1

	£
List price of goods	380.00
Less: 10% trade discount	(38.00)
	342.00
Less: 4% settlement discount	(13.68)
Amount on which VAT to be calculated	328.32
VAT at 17.5% × £328.32	57.45

Activity 2

1   VAT on 6 metre hosepipes £9.04 (£51.68 × 17.5% = £9.044)

2   VAT on 12 metre hosepipes £24.27 (£138.72 × 17.5% = £24.276)

3   VAT £189.78 (£1,084.50 × 17.5% = £189.787)

All rounded down to the nearest penny.

Activity 3

1   15 July – invoice within 14 days after basic tax point (delivery date 10 July)

2   12 August – goods invoiced before delivery

3   4 September – payment received before delivery

4   13 September – delivery date

VAT accounting schemes

Introduction

This chapter deals with VAT accounting. There are several special schemes available for small businesses. These schemes have a number of advantages. They can reduce administration (annual accounting and flat rate scheme) or improve cash flow (cash accounting).

You should pay particular attention to which businesses are eligible and the reasons why a business might join one of these schemes.

KNOWLEDGE

Explain the requirements and the frequency of reporting for the following VAT schemes: annual accounting; cash accounting; flat rate scheme; standard scheme (1.7)

SKILLS

Complete accurately and submit a VAT return within the statutory time limits along with any associated payments (1.5)

CONTENTS

1 Standard scheme
2 Annual accounting
3 Cash accounting
4 Flat rate scheme

1 Standard scheme

1.1 Return periods

All registered traders have to complete a VAT return every return period. Information to complete the return is taken from sales and purchase information – usually from daybook totals. Any amounts of VAT due must be paid over to HMRC or a claim made for VAT to be reimbursed.

Return periods are normally 3 months, but traders who regularly receive repayments may elect for monthly return periods.

1.2 Submission of returns

Returns must normally be submitted one month after the end of the return period. Traders who submit their returns online, rather than using a paper return, usually get an extra 7 days to submit.

From April 2010 most businesses have to submit their returns online.

Completion of VAT returns is dealt with in chapter 6.

1.3 Payment of VAT

The due date for payment of VAT depends on whether the trader is paying by sending a cheque through the post or paying electronically.

Postal payments can only be made with paper VAT returns and payment is due at the same time as the return, i.e. one month after the end of the return period.

Electronic payments **must** be made if returns are submitted online and **may** be made when paper returns are submitted. The payment date is normally 7 days later than for a postal payment. (Note, if this falls on a weekend or Bank holiday, the payment must reach HMRC by the previous working day).

 Example

Jonas has a quarterly return period to 30 April.

If Jonas submits a paper VAT return it must be with HMRC by 31 May. If he submits electronically he will have until 7 June to submit.

If Jonas submits a paper return he can send a cheque with his return to arrive by 31 May. Otherwise he must pay electronically by 7 June.

1.4 Other schemes

There are a number of special schemes for accounting for VAT. These are designed to help small businesses by reducing administration and may improve cash flow. The schemes which you must know about are:

- annual accounting
- cash accounting
- the flat rate scheme.

There are also special schemes for retailers and businesses that sell second–hand goods. However you do not need to know details of these.

2 Annual accounting scheme

2.1 Purpose of the scheme

Smaller businesses may find it costly or inconvenient to prepare the normal four quarterly VAT returns.

An 'annual' accounting scheme is available whereby a single VAT return is filed for a 12-month period (normally the accounting period of the business). This helps relieve the burden of administration.

2.2 How the scheme works

Only one VAT return is submitted each year, but VAT payments must still be made regularly. The scheme works as follows:

- The annual return must be filed within 2 months of the end of the annual return period

- Normally, nine payments on account of the VAT liability for the year are made at the end of months 4 to 12 of the year. Each payment represents 10% of the VAT liability for the previous year.

- A new business will base its payments on an estimate of the VAT liability for the year.

- Businesses may apply to HMRC to agree quarterly payments on account instead of the normal nine monthly payments. In this case, the payments will be 25% of the VAT liability for the previous year and will be made by the ends of months 4, 7 and 10.

- A balancing payment or repayment is made when the return is filed.

- All payments must be made electronically.

2.3 Conditions for the annual accounting scheme

The scheme is aimed at smaller businesses.

- Businesses can join the scheme provided their taxable turnover (excluding VAT and the sale of capital assets) expected in the next 12 months is no more than £1,350,000.

- The business must be up-to-date with its VAT returns.

- Businesses must leave the scheme if their estimated taxable turnover (excluding VAT) for the next 12 months is more than £1,600,000.

2.4 Who might use the scheme?

The scheme is useful to businesses that want to:

- reduce administration because only one VAT return is needed instead of four.

- fix their VAT payments in advance, at least for their nine monthly or three quarterly payments. This is useful for budgeting cash flow.

It is not useful if:

- the business receives repayments as only one repayment per year will be received.

- the business turnover decreases, as then the interim payments might be higher than under the standard scheme and the business will have to wait until they submit the VAT return to get any repayment due.

 Activity 1

Jump Ltd applies to use the annual accounting scheme from 1 January 20X1. The company's net VAT liability for the year ended 31 December 20X0 was £3,600.00.

The actual net VAT liability for the year ended 31 December 20X1 is £3,820.00.

1   When must Jump Ltd's VAT return be filed?

    A   31 December 20X1
    B   31 January 20X2
    C   28 February 20X2
    D   31 March 20X2

2   Which ONE of the following statements about Jump Ltd's payment of VAT during the year ended 31 December 20X1 is true? Assume Jump Ltd has not chosen quarterly payments.

A   Jump Ltd must make nine monthly payments of £360.00
B   Jump Ltd must make nine monthly payments of £382.00
C   Jump Ltd must make twelve monthly payments of £300.00
D   Jump Ltd must make twelve monthly payments of £318.33

3   What is the balancing payment/repayment due from/to Jump Ltd when their VAT return for the year ended 31 December 20X1 is filed?

3   Cash accounting

3.1   How the scheme works

Normally VAT is accounted for on the basis of invoices issued and received in a return period. Accordingly:

- Output VAT is paid to HMRC by reference to the period in which the tax point occurs (usually the delivery or invoice date), regardless of whether payment has been received from the customer.

- Input VAT is reclaimed from HMRC by reference to the invoices received in the return period, even if payment has not been made to the supplier.

However, under the cash accounting scheme a business accounts for VAT on the basis of the time when payment is actually received from customers or made to suppliers. The tax point becomes the date of receipt or payment.

If registered under the scheme invoices will still be sent to customers and received from suppliers but the key record that must be kept is a cash book. This should summarise all the payments made and received and have a **separate column for VAT.**

3.2   Conditions

As with annual accounting, the scheme is aimed at smaller businesses. The conditions are:

- The trader's VAT returns must be up-to-date and they must have no convictions for VAT offences or penalties for dishonest conduct.

- Estimated taxable turnover, excluding VAT and sales of capital assets, must not exceed £1,350,000 for the next year.

- Once in the scheme, a trader must leave once their annual taxable turnover, excluding VAT, exceeds £1,600,000.

3.3 Advantages and disadvantages

Advantages	Disadvantages
• Businesses selling on credit do not have to pay output VAT to HMRC until they receive it from customers.	• Input tax cannot be claimed until the invoice is paid. This delays recovery of input VAT.
• This gives automatic bad debt relief because if the customer does not pay, then the VAT on their invoice is not paid over to HMRC. Cash flow is improved.	• Not suitable for businesses with a lot of cash sales or zero – rated supplies. Using cash accounting in these situations would simply cause a delay in the recovery of input VAT.

Activity 2

Would each of the following businesses benefit from joining the cash accounting scheme? Select Yes or No for each business.

1   JB Ltd which operates a retail shop selling directly to the public. All sales are for cash and all purchases are made on credit. JB Ltd's supplies are all standard rated.   YES/NO

2   Amber and Co, which manufactures and sells computer printers to other businesses. This is a standard rated business and all sales and purchases are made on credit.   YES/NO

3   John Smith, a sole trader who manufactures children's shoes and sells them to retailers. This is a zero-rated activity and all sales and purchases are made on credit.   YES/NO

4 The flat rate scheme

4.1 Purpose of the scheme

The optional flat rate scheme is aimed at simplifying the way in which very small businesses calculate their VAT liability.

4.2 How the scheme works

Under the flat rate scheme, a business **calculates its VAT liability** by simply applying a flat rate percentage to total turnover. This removes the need to calculate and record output and input VAT. In some cases it can save the business money.

- The flat rate percentage is applied to the gross (VAT inclusive) **total turnover** figure. This includes standard rated, zero rated and exempt supplies. No input VAT is recovered.

- The total turnover is obtained using one of three methods:

  (a) basic turnover method – uses the normal tax point rules to determine in which VAT period the turnover falls

  (b) cash based turnover – bases VAT on the supplies for which customers have paid during the period

  (c) retailer's turnover method – from daily takings as received, typically totals from till records are used.

- The percentage varies according to the type of trade in which the business is involved. In their first year in the scheme a business gets a 1% discount on their normal percentage. If you need to know a percentage in the assessment it will be given to you.

- A **VAT invoice must still be issued** to customers and VAT charged at the appropriate rate.

- A VAT account must still be maintained.

- The flat rate scheme is **only** used to calculate the VAT due to HMRC.

- The flat rate scheme can be used together with the annual accounting scheme.

4.3 Conditions for the scheme

In order to join the scheme, the **taxable** turnover of the business, (excluding VAT), for the next 12 months must not be expected to exceed £150,000.

Once in the scheme, a business can stay in until their tax inclusive turnover (including taxable and exempt income) for the previous 12 months exceeds £225,000.

 Example

Simon runs a business selling computer supplies. He has joined the flat rate scheme.

If the flat rate percentage for this type of business is 12%, how much VAT should Simon pay over for the quarter ended 30 June 20X0 when his turnover (including VAT) is £39,000?

Solution

£4,680.00 (£39,000 × 12%)

4.4 Advantages and disadvantages of the flat rate scheme

The advantages of the scheme include the following:

- A business does not have to record the VAT charged on each individual sale and purchase.

- Easier administration as the business does not have to decide which input VAT can be reclaimed and which cannot.

- The business gets a discount of 1% in the first year.

- The business may pay less VAT than using the standard method.

- The business has certainty as the percentage of turnover that has to be paid over as VAT is known in advance.

- There is less chance of making a mistake in calculating VAT.

The percentage used in flat rate accounting is fixed for particular trade sectors and takes into account the mix of standard rated, zero rated and exempt sales made by the average business in that sector. The scheme may not be suitable for businesses which do not have the same mix as an average business. In particular it would not be suitable for:

- businesses that regularly receive repayments under standard VAT accounting

- businesses that buy a higher proportion of standard rated items than others in their trade sector as they would not be able to reclaim the input VAT on these purchases

- businesses that make a higher proportion of zero rated or exempt sales than others in their trade.

 Activity 3

In the year ended 31 December 20X0, Apple Ltd has annual sales of £70,000, all of which are standard rated and to the general public. The company incurs standard rated expenses of £4,500 per annum. These figures include VAT at 17.5%.

1 Select which of the following gives Apple Ltd's liability using the standard method.

A	£11,462.50
B	£9,755.31
C	£11,579.78
D	£9,638.03

2 Select which of the following gives Apple Ltd's VAT liability using the flat rate method assuming a percentage of 9%.

A	£12,250.00
B	£10,425.53
C	£6,300.00
D	£5,895.00

5 Test your knowledge

 Test your knowledge

Having completed Chapter 4 you should now be able to attempt:

Practice Activities 24 to 30.

6 Summary

Clearly it is important for a business to know when they have to complete VAT returns and pay over VAT. The normal pattern is to complete returns and pay over VAT quarterly or monthly. This is the case unless the business has chosen annual accounting which is one of the special schemes aimed at smaller businesses.

Annual accounting gives the advantages of only one annual VAT return and fixed regular VAT payments. The turnover limits for the scheme are the same as for cash accounting.

Cash accounting changes the normal tax point rules and allows the business to pay over VAT when they actually receive the cash from their customers rather than the delivery or invoice date. This gives automatic bad debt relief but has the disadvantage that input VAT can only be claimed when suppliers are paid.

The flat rate scheme is aimed at simplifying VAT accounting for the very small business. The amount of VAT payable is determined by simply applying a fixed percentage to the VAT inclusive turnover of the business. However it is important to remember that the business still has to comply with the rules about issuing tax invoices.

Answers to chapter activities

Activity 1

1   C   28 February 20X2 – 2 months after the year end.

2   A   Nine monthly payments must be made, each of which are 10% of the VAT liability for the previous year.

3   The balancing payment will be £580.00 (£3,820.00 – £360.00 × 9)

Activity 2

1   NO   As sales are all in cash, the adoption of the cash accounting scheme would not affect the time when output tax would be accounted for but would delay the recovery of input tax until the business had paid its suppliers.

2   YES The business would benefit because it would only account for output VAT when the customer paid. Even though the recovery of input VAT would be delayed until the suppliers were paid, the amount of input VAT is likely to be less than output VAT so the business does gain a net cash flow advantage.

3   NO   As the sales are zero rated no output tax is payable. The adoption of the cash accounting scheme would simply delay the recovery of input VAT until the suppliers were paid.

Activity 3

1   B   £9.755.31 (17.5/117.5 (£70,000 – £4,500))

2   C   £6,300.00 (9% × £70,000)

VAT errors and penalties

5

Introduction

This chapter is a short one explaining what happens if a business does not abide by all the VAT regulations.

Correction of errors is also covered. This is an important topic and will often be tested in the assessment task dealing with the actual completion of a VAT return.

KNOWLEDGE
Recognise the implications and penalties for the organisation resulting from failure to abide by VAT regulations including the late submission of VAT returns (1.8)

SKILLS
Make adjustments and declarations for any errors or omissions identified in previous VAT periods (1.4)

CONTENTS
1 Tax avoidance and evasion
2 Penalties
3 Default surcharge

1 Tax avoidance and evasion

1.1 Tax avoidance

Tax avoidance means arranging your tax affairs using legal means, so that you pay less tax. Individuals and businesses can reduce their tax bills by claiming all the reliefs and allowances to which they are entitled. Sometimes a transaction can be timed to give maximum tax advantage.

Tax avoidance is legal.

1.2 Tax evasion

However, tax evasion is a criminal offence. Tax evasion means using illegal means to reduce tax due. Typically this might be through concealing a source of income, deliberately understating income or overclaiming expenses and reliefs. VAT could be evaded by underdeclaring or concealing outputs and output tax or by overstating inputs and hence overclaiming input tax.

VAT evasion is a criminal offence, but in many cases HMRC prefer to claim penalties and interest rather than pursue cases through the courts.

2 Penalties

2.1 Introduction

VAT has many regulations with which a business must comply. As mentioned in chapter 1, HMRC have powers to check whether a business is keeping to the rules.

- HMRC make occasional control visits to check that returns are correct.

- HMRC have the power to enter business premises and inspect records and documents.

If a business fails to comply with VAT regulations they will usually receive a penalty (fine). The amount of the penalty varies according to the offence, but in recent years HMRC has been working to produce a standard penalty system.

For your assessment, you need to know the main principles of the enforcement regime but not the fine detail.

2.2 Summary of main penalties

Offence	Penalty
Failure to register	Standard penalty plus all VAT due from date registration should have taken place
Incorrect return	Standard penalty plus error must be corrected
Late returns and/or late payment	Default surcharge

2.3 Failure to register

Registration rules were dealt with in Chapter 2.

If a business fails to register when it should, then it can be asked to pay over all the VAT due since the date they should have registered, plus a penalty can be levied.

The penalty is determined by the standard penalty regime which applies across all taxes and is a percentage of the VAT outstanding. The percentage to use varies from 0% for genuine mistakes up to 100% for deliberate and concealed actions. The penalty can be reduced if the trader cooperates with HMRC.

2.4 Incorrect return

If a trader makes an error in a VAT return which leads to net VAT payable being understated this must be corrected (see below). A net VAT error is calculated as the difference between VAT due to HMRC less any VAT claimable by the trader.

Note that the amount of any errors or omissions will be given in the assessment.

Example

Bishop is a registered trader who prepares VAT returns quarterly. He discovers that in his previous quarter he entered VAT output tax on his return as £56,792.00 when it should have been £65,972.00. He also entered input tax as £45,510.00 when it should have been £45,150.00.

He also discovers that he has not reclaimed the VAT of £3,450.00 on the purchase of a new milling machine.

What is the net VAT error?

Solution

	£
Output tax understated (£65,972.00 – £56,792.00)	9,180.00
Input tax overstated (£45,510.00 – £45,150.00)	360.00
Input tax understated – not claimed on machine	(3,450.00)
	————
Net VAT error	6,090.00
	————

A penalty under the standard penalty regime may be charged. This will be a percentage of the net VAT understated, and as for late registration, it varies from 0% to 100% of the error.

In addition, interest may be charged.

2.5 Correcting errors – voluntary disclosure

If a trader discovers that they have made an error in an earlier VAT return then they must try to correct it as soon as possible. There are two methods of correction depending on the size of error.

• Include on next VAT return

• Include on VAT form 652 (or by letter if no form available).

Include on next VAT return	Submit on form 652
Errors can be corrected on the next VAT return if they are:	Errors must be separately disclosed if they:
• No more than £10,000	• Exceed £50,000
• Between £10,000 and £50,000 but no more than 1% of turnover for the current return period (specifically the figure included in box 6 of the return – see Chapter 6)	• Exceed £10,000 and are more than 1% of the turnover for the current return period (figure in Box 6 of the return)

Activity 13

You are given the following information about the net errors and turnover of four businesses. For each of them, indicate whether they can correct the error on the next VAT return or whether separate disclosure is required. Tick ONE box on EACH line.

Net error £	Turnover £	Include in VAT return	Separate disclosure
4,500.00	100,000	✓	
12,000.00	250,000	✓	✓
30,000.00	3,500,000	✓	
60,000.00	10,000,000		✓

2.6 Errors found by HMRC

An error may be discovered by HMRC, for example during a VAT control visit. In this case HMRC may issue a discovery assessment (i.e. a demand) to collect any VAT due.

Normally HMRC have up to 4 years after the end of the return period in which the error occurred to issue an assessment. This is extended to 6 years if the error was due to careless behaviour and to 20 years for deliberate behaviour (such as fraud).

HMRC can also issue a penalty under the standard penalty regime and charge interest on the unpaid VAT. Any penalty is likely to be higher than if the trader found the error themselves and voluntarily disclosed it.

3 Default surcharge

3.1 Surcharge liability notice

If a trader commits a **default** by submitting their VAT return late or paying their VAT late, HMRC will serve a **surcharge liability notice** on the trader. This identifies a surcharge period which runs until 12 months after the end of the period for which the trader is in default.

Example

Jolene submits her paper return for the quarter ended 30 June 20X6 on 15 August 20X6 but pays her VAT electronically on 3 August 20X6.

As this is a late return, a surcharge liability notice will be issued by HMRC which will cover a period up to 30 June 20X7.

3.2 Effect of surcharge liability notice

The surcharge liability notice acts as a warning to the trader. If they commit a further default within the surcharge period then:

(i)   the surcharge period is extended so it now ends 12 months after the end of the new default period and,

(ii)   if the default is a late VAT payment (rather than just a late VAT return), then the trader is charged a **surcharge** penalty which is a fixed percentage of the VAT overdue.

The process is repeated if the trader commits further defaults within the surcharge period, with increasing levels of penalty charged. Hence the trader needs to stay free of defaults for twelve months to come out of the default surcharge system.

For assessment purposes you are not expected to know how the amount of the surcharge is calculated or what happens if a further default arises in the surcharge period.

3.3 Small businesses

Small businesses (with turnover up to £150,000 per annum) will not receive a surcharge liability notice on their first default but will be sent a letter offering them help and advice. However, if they default again within the next 12 months, they will be issued a surcharge liability notice and suffer the same consequences as other businesses.

3.4 Reasonable excuse

A surcharge liability notice will not be issued if the trader has a **reasonable excuse** for submitting their return or paying their VAT late.

Examples of reasonable excuse include:

*   Computer breakdown just before or during the preparation of the return or loss of records due to fire or flood.

*   Illness of an employee who prepares the return where no one else can do the work.

- Sudden cash crisis such as loss of cash due to theft or major customer becoming insolvent.

4 Test your knowledge

 Test your knowledge

Having completed Chapter 5 you should now be able to attempt:

Practice Activities 31 to 33.

5 Summary

It is important to know the difference between tax avoidance and evasion as one is illegal and one is not.

VAT is a self assessed tax – that is traders calculate their own VAT liability. HMRC have powers to visit businesses and check that they are complying with the rules. If not, penalties can be charged.

For your assessment you need to know the main principles of the enforcement regime, but not the fine detail.

Three main penalties have been discussed in this chapter, late registration, incorrect returns and late submission of VAT returns and payments.

Late registration and errors in returns are dealt with under the common penalty regime. The penalty is not a fixed monetary amount but is determined as a percentage of VAT outstanding. The percentage varies according to the trader's actions and level of cooperation.

The default surcharge applies to late returns and payments. The examiner has stated that you need to know what triggers a surcharge liability notice but you will not be expected to know how the amount of the surcharge is calculated.

Correction of errors is an important area. You will normally be asked to deal with the correction of errors in the assessment task involving completion of the VAT return.

Answers to chapter activities

 Activity 13

1   Error £4,500.00 – include on VAT return as below £10,000

2   Error £12,000.00 – separate disclosure is needed as this error is more than £10,000 and is more than 1% of turnover

3   Error £30,000.00 – can be included on VAT return as between £10,000 and £50,000 and less than 1% of turnover

4   Error £60,000.00 – must be separately disclosed as more than £50,000

VAT Returns

Introduction

In the final chapter of this study text we are going to conclude our VAT studies by looking at how to complete a VAT return correctly and on time. Businesses must complete a VAT return (a VAT 100 form) at the end of each quarter. The purpose of a VAT return is to summarise the transactions of a business for a period. In an assessment you will be required to complete an organisation's VAT return so that it is ready for authorisation and despatch.

KNOWLEDGE

Recognise different types of inputs and outputs (1.5)

Identify how different types of supply are classified for VAT purposes (1.6)

SKILLS

Correctly identify and extract relevant data for a specific period from the accounting system (1.1)

Calculate accurately relevant inputs and outputs (1.2)

Calculate accurately the VAT due to, or from, the relevant tax authority (1.3)

Make adjustments and declarations for any errors or omissions identified in previous VAT periods (1.4)

Complete accurately and submit a VAT return within the statutory time limits along with any associated payments (1.5)

Inform managers of the impact that the VAT payment may have on the company cash flow and financial forecasts (2.1)

CONTENTS

1 The VAT return
2 Imports and exports
3 Completing the VAT return
4 Communicating VAT information

1 The VAT return

1.1 Introduction

The tax period for VAT is **three months**, or one month for taxpayers who choose to make monthly returns (normally taxpayers who receive regular refunds).

The taxpayer must complete a **VAT return at the end of each quarter**. The return summarises all the transactions for the period.

1.2 Timing of the VAT return

The taxpayer must make the return within one month of the end of the tax period. The taxable person must send the amount due at the same time (i.e. output tax collected less input tax deducted).

For more detail on VAT returns and payments refer back to Chapter 4.

If VAT is due from HM Revenue and Customs the VAT return must still be completed and submitted within one month of the end of the quarter in order to be able to reclaim the amount due.

1.3 What a VAT return looks like

An example of a paper VAT return is given below in section 1.4.

Most businesses have to file their returns online rather than on paper, however the boxes and numbers used for the electronic form are exactly the same.

In the assessment you will have to complete a VAT return which may be a paper return or as shown in section 1.5.

You will only have to complete boxes 1 to 9.

1.4 Paper VAT return

Value Added Tax Return
For the period

For Official Use

Registration number

Period

You could be liable to a financial penalty if your completed return and all the VAT payable are not received by the due date.

Due date:

| For Official Use | |

Your VAT Office telephone number is 0123 4567

Before you fill in this form please read the notes on the back and the VAT Leaflet *'Filling in your VAT return'*. Fill in all boxes clearly in ink and write *'none'* where necessary. Don't put a dash or leave any box blank. If there are no pence write *'00'* in the pence column. Do not enter more than one amount in any box

For official use				
	VAT due in this period on sales and other options	1		
	VAT due in this period on acquisitions from other EC Member states	2		
	Total VAT due (the sum of boxes 1 and 2)	3		
	VAT reclaimed in this period on purchases and other inputs (including acquisitions from the EC)	4		
	Net VAT to be paid to Customs or reclaimed by you (Difference between boxes 3 and 4)	5		
	Total value of sales and all other outputs excluding any VAT. Include your box 8 figure	6		00
	Total value of purchases and all other inputs excluding any VAT. Include your box 9 figures.	7		00
	Total value of all supplies of goods and related services excluding any VAT to other EC Member States	8		00
	Total value of all supplies of goods and related services excluding any VAT, from other EC Member States	9		00

Retail schemes. If you have used any of the schemes in the period covered by this return, enter the relevant letter(s) in this box.

If you are enclosing a payment please tick this box	DECLARATION You or someone on your behalf must sign below.
	I .... declare that the information given (Full name of signatory in BLOCK LETTERS) above is true and complete. Signature .... Date 20 A false declaration can result in prosecution.

1.5   VAT return – online style

VAT due in this period on **sales** and other outputs (Box 1)

VAT due in this period on **acquisitions** from other **EC Member States** (Box 2)

Total VAT due (**the sum of boxes 1 and 2**) (Box 3)

VAT reclaimed in the period on **purchases** and other inputs, including acquisitions from the EC (Box 4)

Net VAT to be paid to HM Revenue & Customs or reclaimed by you (**Difference between boxes 3 and 4**) (Box 5)

Total value of **sales** and all other outputs excluding any VAT. **Include your box 8 figure** (Box 6)

Whole pounds only

Total value of purchases and all other inputs excluding any VAT. **Include your box 9 figure** (Box 7)

Whole pounds only

Total value of all **supplies** of goods and related costs, excluding any VAT, to other **EC Member States** (Box 8)

Whole pounds only

Total value of all **acquisitions** of goods and related costs, excluding any VAT, from other **EC Member States** (Box 9)

Whole pounds only

As you will see there are nine boxes to complete with the relevant figures. Boxes 2, 8 and 9 are to do with supplies of goods and services to other European Community (EC) Member States and acquisitions from EC Member States. Therefore the next section considers how VAT is affected by exports and imports.

2 Imports and Exports

2.1 Introduction

VAT is a tax levied within the European Community (EC). It applies to sales within the EC but not to sales outside the EC (exports).

All purchases made by EC businesses are subject to VAT even if purchased from outside the EC.

The rules for dealing with purchases from outside the EC can be complex, but you only require a broad understanding of how they are dealt with.

2.1 Exports and imports to or from non-EC members

(a) Generally, goods **exported** from the United Kingdom to a non-EC country are zero-rated (i.e. there is no tax charged on them, even if there normally would be) provided there is documentary evidence of the export.

As no VAT needs to be charged, there will be no output tax to include in Box 1. This is the same for all zero-rated sales.

However these export sales **are** included with other sales in Box 6 of the return.

(b) Goods that are imported from outside the EC have to have customs duty paid on them when they enter the country (these are outside the scope of Indirect Tax and are not considered further).

However, goods that would be taxed at the standard rate of VAT if supplied in the United Kingdom are also subject to VAT. The amount payable is based on their value including customs duty. This applies to **all goods** whether or not they are for business use. The aim of the charge is to treat foreign goods in the same way as home-produced goods.

The VAT is paid at the port of entry and the goods will typically not be released until it is paid. If the imported goods are for business use and the business uses them to make taxable supplies, it can reclaim the VAT paid in the usual way as input tax on the VAT return (Box 4).

The cost of the goods purchased (excluding VAT) is included with other purchases in Box 7.

2.2 Exports and imports to and from countries within the EC

When both the exporting and importing country are EC members, the rules differ according to whether the purchaser is a VAT registered business or not.

Note that movements of goods between EC Member States are not known as imports and exports but as **acquisitions** and **dispatches**.

In what follows we refer to HM Revenue and Customs ('HMRC') as the collecting authority, even though in different countries it will have a different name.

(a) Sale to a VAT registered business

When an EC member sells goods to a VAT registered business in another EC country, it is the **buyer** who pays over the VAT to HMRC (or the equivalent in the buyer's country). Provided the seller has the buyer's VAT number, the seller sells the goods zero rated to the buyer. The buyer will then pay VAT to HMRC at the appropriate rate. The buyer can also reclaim the VAT from HMRC.

We can summarise this as follows:

The seller

The seller will supply the goods zero rated.

The seller makes no entries in Boxes 1 to 4 of the VAT return (in common with other zero rated sales).

The seller will enter the value of the sale with other sales in Box 6 **and** enter in Box 8. Note the wording on the form helps you with this.

The buyer

The VAT registered buyer will pay the seller the sale price of the goods (excluding any VAT).

The buyer will enter the VAT output tax in Box 2 of the return and the VAT input tax in Box 4 of the return. Thus, the net amount of VAT the buyer pays to HMRC is nil.

The buyer will also enter the VAT exclusive price of the goods in Box 7 (with the other purchases) and also in Box 9.

(b) Sale to a non-VAT registered buyer

When a sale is made to a non-VAT registered buyer, the seller has to charge VAT at the standard rate. The buyer will pay the VAT inclusive price to the seller. The entries on the return are the same as if selling to a UK customer. These sales will not be included in Box 8.

We can summarise this as follows:

The seller

The seller supplies the goods and charges VAT. The seller enters the VAT in Box 1.

The seller enters the VAT exclusive price in Box 6.

The buyer

The non-VAT registered buyer pays the VAT inclusive price to the seller and of course makes no entries in a VAT return because he is not registered.

Note that if a UK business has a high level of such sales to another EC country, they may have to register for VAT in that other country. This is outside the scope of this unit.

 Example

Trystan runs a UK business selling Welsh handicraft items. He has recently started to sell goods overseas. All the goods he sells are standard rated items. The VAT rate is 17.5%.

In the quarter ended 31 December 20X1 he makes sales as follows:

	£
Sales to UK businesses	40,000
Sales to EC registered businesses	10,500
Sales to EC non registered customers	21,000
Export sales outside the EC	12,400
All these figures exclude VAT.	

What are the figures to include in Boxes 1, 6 and 8?

Solution

		£
Box 1	VAT on standard rated sales	
	17.5% × (£40,000 + £21,000)	10,675.00
Box 6	All sales	
	(£40,000 + £10,500 + £21,000 + £12,400)	83,900
Box 8	Sales to EC businesses	10,500

Example

Bettrys runs a UK business selling standard rated pet accessories. She imports some items from overseas, both from other EC countries and from outside the EC. The VAT rate is 17.5%.

In the quarter ended 31 December 20X1 her purchases are as follows:

	£
Purchases from UK businesses	27,400
Purchases from EC registered businesses	13,700
Purchases from outside the EC	18,800
All these figures exclude VAT.	

What are the figures to include in Boxes 2, 4, 7 and 9?

Solution

		£
Box 2	VAT on acquisitions from other EC countries 17.5% × £13,700	2,397.50
Box 4	VAT reclaimed 17.5% × (£27,400 + £13,700 + £18,800)	10,482.50
Box 7	Total purchases (£27,400 + £13,700 + £18,700)	59,900
Box 9	Purchases from other EC countries	13,700

3 Completing the VAT return

3.1 The VAT account

The main source of information for the VAT return is the VAT account which must be maintained to show the amount that is due to or from HM Revenue and Customs ('HMRC') at the end of each quarter.

It is important to realise that the balance on the VAT account should agree to the balance of VAT payable/reclaimable on the VAT return.

3.2 How the VAT account should look

Given below is a pro-forma of a VAT account as suggested by the VAT Guide.

---

1 April 20X5 to 30 June 20X5

VAT deductible – input tax		VAT payable – output tax	
VAT on purchases		VAT on sales	
April	X	April	X
May	X	May	X
June	X	June	X
VAT on imports	X		
VAT on acquisition from EC	X	VAT on acquisition from EC	X

Adjustments of previous errors
(if within the error limit – see Chapter 5)

Net under claim	X	Net over claim	X
Bad debt relief (see later)	X		
Less: Credit notes received	(X)	Less: Credit notes issued	(X)
	—		—
Total tax deductible	X	Total tax payable	X
	—	Less: total tax deductible	(X)
			—
		Payable to HMRC	X
			—

You will note that the VAT shown is not strictly a double entry account as the VAT on credit notes received is deducted from input tax and the VAT on credit notes issued is deducted from output tax instead of being credited and debited respectively.

3.3 Information required for the VAT return

Boxes 1 to 4 of the VAT return can be fairly easily completed from the information in the VAT account. However, Boxes 6 and 7 require figures for total sales and purchases excluding VAT. This information will need to be extracted from the totals of the accounting records such as sales day book and purchases day book totals. It is also possible that information relating to VAT could be shown in a journal.

Boxes 8 and 9 require figures, excluding VAT, for the value of supplies to other EC Member States and acquisitions from other EC Member States. Therefore the accounting records should be designed in such a way that these figures can also be easily identified.

Activity 1

Panther

You are preparing the VAT return for Panther Alarms Ltd and you must first identify the sources of information for the VAT account.

Here is a list of possible sources of accounting information.

1   Sales day book   *A*
2   Sales returns day book   *C*
3   Bad and doubtful debts account   *J*
4   Purchase returns day book   *F*
5   Drawings account   *I*
6   Purchases day book   *D*
7   Cash book   *E B*
8   Assets account   *G H*
9   Petty cash book   *E*

Select from the list the best sources of information for the following figures by entering a number against each. If you think that the information will be in more than one place then give the number for both.

A   sales

B   cash sales

C   credit notes issued

D   purchases

E   cash purchases

F   credit notes received

G   capital goods sold

H   capital goods purchased

I   goods taken from business for own use

J   bad debt relief

Example

Given below is a VAT account for Thompson Brothers for the second VAT quarter of 20X5.

Thompson Brothers Ltd

1 April 20X5 to 30 June 20X5

VAT deductible – input tax		VAT payable – output tax	
VAT on purchases	£	*VAT on sales*	£
April	525.00	April	875.00
May	350.00	May	1,750.00
June	350.00	June	700.00
	1,225.00		3,325.00
EC acquisitions	210.00		210.00

Other adjustements

Less: Credit notes received	(17.50)	Less: Credit notes issued	(105.00)
Total tax deductible	1,417.50	Total tax payable	3,430.00
		Less: total tax deductible	(1,417.50)
		Payable to HM Revenue and Customs	2,012.50

You are also given the summarised totals from the day books for the three-month period:

Sales Day Book

	Net £	VAT £	Total £
Standard rated	19,000.00	3,325.00	22,325.00
Zero rated	800.00	–	800.00
EC Member States	1,500.00	–	1,500.00

Sales Returns Day Book

	Net £	VAT £	Total £
Standard rated	600.00	105.00	705.00
Zero rated	40.00	–	40.00
EC Member States	–	–	–

Purchases Day Book

	Net £	VAT £	Total £
Standard rated	7,000.00	1,225.00	8,225.00
Zero rated	2,000.00	–	2,000.00
EC Member States	1,200.00	210.00	1,410.00

Purchases Returns Day Book

	Net £	VAT £	Total £
Standard rated	100.00	17.50	117.50
Zero rated	–	–	–
EC Member States	–	–	–

We are now in a position to complete the VAT return.

Solution

Step 1

Fill in Box 1 with the VAT on sales less the VAT on credit notes issued – this can be taken either from the VAT account or from the day book summaries: £3,325 – £105 = £3,220.00.

Note that the figures in Boxes 1-5 should include pence so put '00' if there are no pence in the total.

Step 2

Fill in Box 2 with the VAT payable on acquisitions from other EC Member States – this figure of £210.00 can be taken either from the VAT account or from the Purchases Day Book.

Note that this figure will be included here on the VAT return as output tax payable to HM Revenue and Customs and also in Box 4 as input tax reclaimable.

Step 3

Complete Box 3 with the total of Boxes 1 and 2: £3,220.00 + £210.00 = £3,430.00.

Step 4

Fill in Box 4 with the total of VAT on all purchases (including acquisitions from EC Member States) less the total VAT on any credit notes received. These figures can either be taken from the VAT account or from the day book totals: £1,225.00 + £210.00 – £17.50 = £1,417.50.

Step 5

Complete Box 5 by deducting the figure in Box 4 from the total in Box 3: £3,430.00 – £1,417.50 = £2,012.50. This is the amount due to HM

Revenue and Customs and should equal the balance on the VAT account.

If the Box 4 figure is larger than the Box 3 total then there is more input tax reclaimable than output tax to pay – this means that this is the amount being reclaimed from HM Revenue and Customs.

For a paper return, a negative figure like a repayment should be put in brackets. For an online return a negative figure should have a negative sign in front and no brackets.

Step 6

Fill in Box 6 with the VAT exclusive figure of all sales less credit notes issued – this information will come from the day books – this figure includes sales to EC Member States: £19,000 + £800 + £1,500 – £600 – £40 = £20,660.

Note that this figure includes zero-rated supplies and any exempt supplies that are made.

Note that the figures in boxes 6-9 should be whole pounds only (pence will already be completed as '00' on a paper return).

Step 7

Fill in Box 7 with the VAT exclusive total of all purchases less credit notes received – again this will be taken from the day books: £7,000 + £2,000 + £1,200 – £100 = £10,100.

Step 8

Fill in Box 8 with the VAT exclusive total of all supplies made to EC Member States (less any credit notes) – this figure is taken from the Sales Day Book: £1,500.

Step 9

Fill in Box 9 with the VAT exclusive total of all acquisitions from other EC Member States (less any credit notes) – this figure is taken from the Purchases Day Book: £1,200.

Note that if there is no entry for any box then 'none' should be written in the box for a paper return and 0 for an online return

Step 10

If VAT is due to HM Revenue and Customs then payment must be made in accordance with the usual time limits. For assessment purposes you may be asked to state the payment date, or draft an email advising when this amount will be paid.

Note that in the completed paper return below, the name, address and VAT registration number have been included for illustrative purposes.

Value Added Tax Return
For the period 1/4/X5 TO 30/6/X5

For Official Use

Thompson Brothers Ltd
Arnold House
Parkway
Keele
KE4 8VS

Registration number	Period
165 4385 32	20X5

You could be liable to a financial penalty if your completed return and all the VAT payable are not received by the due date.

Due date: 31 July 20X5

Your VAT Office telephone number is 0123 4567

For Official Use	

Before you fill in this form please read the notes on the back and the VAT Leaflet *'Filling in your VAT return'*. Fill in all boxes clearly in ink and write 'none' where necessary. Don't put a dash or leave any box blank. If there are no pence write '00' in the pence column. Do not enter more than one amount in any box

For official use				
	VAT due in this period on sales and other options	1	3,220	00
	VAT due in this period on acquisitions from other EC Member states	2	210	00
	Total VAT due (the sum of boxes 1 and 2)	3	3,430	00
	VAT reclaimed in this period on purchases and other inputs (including acquisitions from the EC)	4	1,417	50
	Net VAT to be paid to Customs or reclaimed by you (Difference between boxes 3 and 4)	5	2,012	50
	Total value of sales and all other outputs excluding any VAT. Include your box 8 figure	6	20,660	00
	Total value of purchases and all other inputs excluding any VAT. Include your box 9 figures.	7	10,100	00
	Total value of all supplies of goods and related services excluding any VAT to other EC Member States	8	1,500	00
	Total value of all supplies of goods and related services excluding any VAT, from other EC Member States	9	1,200	00

Retail schemes. If you have used any of the schemes in the period covered by this return, enter the relevant letter(s) in this box.

If you are enclosing a payment please tick this box

✓

DECLARATION You or someone on your behalf must sign below.

I ....A Thompson...................... declare that the information given
(Full name of signatory in BLOCK LETTERS)
above is true and complete.
Signature .... Date   20
A false declaration can result in prosecution.

VAT 100 (full)   PT1 (April 2004)

If the business makes sales or purchases for cash then the relevant net and VAT figures from the cash receipts and payments books should also be included on the VAT return.

Activity 2

Given below is a summary of the day books of a business for the three months ended 31 March 20X1. The business is called Long Supplies Ltd and trades from Vale House, Lilly Road, Trent, TR5 2KL. The VAT registration number of the business is 285 3745 12.

Sales Day Book	Net £	VAT £	Total £
Standard-rate	15,485.60	2,709.98	18,195.58
Zero-rated	1,497.56	–	1,497.56

Sales Returns Day Book	Net £	VAT £	Total £
Standard-rate	1,625.77	284.50	1,910.27
Zero-rated	106.59	–	106.59

Purchase Day Book	Net £	VAT £	Total £
Standard-rate	8,127.45	1,422.30	9,549.75
Zero-rated	980.57	–	980.57
EC Member States	669.04	117.08	786.12

Purchases Returns Day Book	Net £	VAT £	Total £
Standard-rate	935.47	163.70	1,099.17
Zero-rated	80.40	–	80.40
EC Member States	–	–	–

Required

(a) Write up the VAT account to reflect these figures.

(b) Complete the VAT return given.

(a) Proforma VAT account for completion

	£		£
VAT on purchases	1539.38	VAT on sales	
EC acquisitions		EC acquisitions	
Less:credit notes received		Less: credit notes issued	
Total tax deductible		Total tax payable	
		Less: total tax deductible	
		Payable to HMRC	

Proforma VAT return for completion

VAT due in this period on **sales** and other outputs (Box 1)

VAT due in this period on **acquisitions** from other **EC Member States** (Box 2)

Total VAT due (**the sum of boxes 1 and 2**) (Box 3)

VAT reclaimed in the period on **purchases** and other inputs, including acquisitions from the EC (Box 4)

Net VAT to be paid to HM Revenue & Customs or reclaimed by you (**Difference between boxes 3 and 4**) (Box 5)

Total value of **sales** and all other outputs excluding any VAT. **Include your box 8 figure** (Box 6)

Whole pounds only

Total value of purchases and all other inputs excluding any VAT. **Include your box 9 figure** (Box 7)

Whole pounds only

Total value of all **supplies** of goods and related costs, excluding any VAT, to other **EC Member States** (Box 8)

Whole pounds only

Total value of all **acquisitions** of goods and related costs, excluding any VAT, from other **EC Member States** (Box 9)

Whole pounds only

3.4 VAT: Adjustment of previous errors

You will notice in the pro-forma VAT account that there are entries for net under claims and net over claims. Net errors made in previous VAT returns which are below the disclosure threshold can be adjusted for on the VAT return through the VAT account.

The error threshold was discussed in Chapter 5. As a reminder errors can be corrected on the next VAT return if they are:

- No more than £10,000

- Between £10,000 and £50,000 but no more than 1% of turnover for the current return period (specifically the figure included in box 6 of the return)

The one single figure for net errors will then be entered as additional input tax in Box 4 if there has been an earlier net under claim of VAT and as additional output tax in Box 1 if the net error was a net over claim in a previous return.

3.5 Errors above the threshold

The VAT office should be informed immediately either by a letter or on Form VAT 652. This is known as voluntary disclosure. The information provided to the VAT office should be:

- how the error happened

- the amount of the error

- the VAT period in which it occurred

- whether the error was involving input or output tax

- how you worked out the error

- whether the error is in favour of the business or HM Revenue and Customs.

3.6 VAT: Bad debt relief

You will notice that there is an entry in the pro-forma VAT account for bad debt relief as additional input tax.

When a supplier invoices a customer for an amount including VAT, the supplier must pay the VAT to HM Revenue and Customs. If the customer then fails to pay the debt, the supplier's position is that he has paid output VAT which he has never collected. This is obviously unfair, and the system allows him to recover such amounts.

Suppliers cannot issue credit notes to recover VAT on bad debts.

Instead, the business must make an **adjustment through the VAT return**. The business can reclaim VAT already paid over if:

- output tax was paid on the original supply

- six months have elapsed between the date payment was due (or the date of supply if later) and the date of the VAT return, and

- the debt has been written off as a bad debt in the accounting records.

If the business receives a **repayment of the debt later**, it must make an adjustment to the VAT relief claimed.

The bad debt relief is entered in box 4 of the return along with the VAT on purchases.

Be very careful when computing the VAT on the bad debt. The amount of the bad debt will be VAT inclusive, because the amount the debtor owes is the amount that includes VAT. To calculate the VAT you have to multiply the bad debt by 17.5/117.5 (or 7/47) for the standard VAT rate of 17.5%.

Example

A business has made purchases of £237,000 (net of VAT) in the VAT quarter and has written off a bad debt of £750. They also have a net under claim of VAT of £1,250.00 from earlier periods.

Calculate the figure that will be entered on the VAT return for the quarter in Box 4.

Solution

	£	£
Purchases (net of VAT)	237,000	
VAT thereon (237,000 × 0.175)		41,475.00
Bad debt	750	
VAT thereon (750 × 17.5/117.5)		111.70
Net underclaim of VAT		1,250.00
		————
Total VAT for Box 4		42,836.70
		————

---

4 Communicating VAT information

4.1 Advising managers of the impact of VAT payments

Once the return has been completed it must be submitted to HMRC and any VAT owing paid over to HMRC. Most businesses submit and pay electronically.

In your assessment you may be asked to draft/complete a short email to the financial accountant or another manager, giving the details of the return submission and the amount payable or receivable. It will be important for the financial accountant, (or other person responsible for managing the business cash), to know when the payment will be made, so that they can make sure that the funds are available in the bank account at the correct time.

> ### Example
>
> To: Financial Accountant
>
> From: Dawn Jones
>
> Date: 17 April 20X1
>
> Subject: VAT return
>
> I have completed the VAT return for the quarter ended 31 March 20X1. The amount of VAT payable will be £23,561.42.
>
> This will be paid electronically by 7 May 20X1.
>
> If you need any further information please contact me.
>
> Best wishes
>
> Dawn (Junior Accountant)

5 Test your knowledge

Test your knowledge

Having completed Chapter 6 you should now be able to attempt:

Practice Activities 34 to 41

6 Summary

In this final chapter the actual completion of the VAT return was considered. A business should keep a VAT account which summarises all of the VAT from the accounting records and this can be used to complete the first five boxes on the VAT return. The figure for VAT due to or from HM Revenue and Customs on the VAT return should equal the balance on the VAT account.

In order to complete the remaining boxes on the VAT return information will be required from the accounting records of the business, normally in the form of the day books.

As well as completing the VAT return you will need to be able to advise the relevant person of the payment or repayment needed.

Answers to chapter activities

Activity 1

Panther

A	Sales	1
B	Cash sales	7
C	Credit notes issued	2
D	Purchases	6
E	Cash purchases	7 and 9
F	Credit notes received	4
G	Capital goods sold	8 or 1 if it is an analysed sales day book
H	Capital goods purchased	8 or 6 (if analysed)
I	Goods for own use	1 and 5
J	Bad debt relief	3

Activity 2

Part (a)

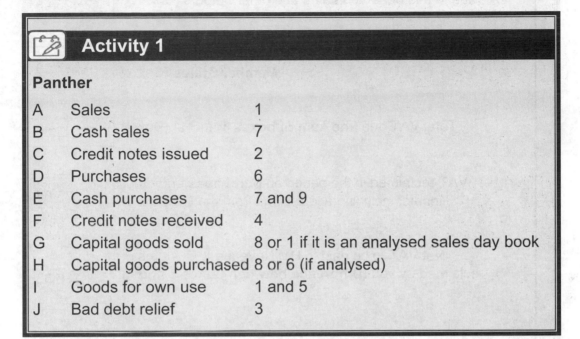

Long Supplies Ltd
VAT account 1 January to 31 March 20X1

	£		£
VAT on purchases	1,422.30	VAT on sales	2,709.98
EC acquisitions	117.08	EC acquisitions	117.08
	1,539.38		2,827.06
Less:credit notes received	(163.70)	Less: credit notes issued	(284.50)
Total tax deductible	1,375.68	Total tax payable	2,542.56
		Less: total tax deductible	(1,375.68)
		Payable to HM Revenue and Customs	1,166.88

Part (b)

VAT due in this period on **sales** and other outputs (Box 1)	2,425.48
VAT due in this period on **acquisitions** from other **EC Member States** (Box 2)	117.08
Total VAT due (**the sum of boxes 1 and 2**) (Box 3)	2,542.56
VAT reclaimed in the period on **purchases** and other inputs, including acquisitions from the EC (Box 4)	1,375.68
Net VAT to be paid to HM Revenue & Customs or reclaimed by you (**Difference between boxes 3 and 4**) (Box 5)	1,166.88
Total value of **sales** and all other outputs excluding any VAT. **Include your box 8 figure** (Box 6)	15,251 Whole pounds only
Total value of purchases and all other inputs excluding any VAT. **Include your box 9 figure** (Box 7)	8,761 Whole pounds only
Total value of all **supplies** of goods and related costs, excluding any VAT, to other **EC Member States** (Box 8)	0 Whole pounds only
Total value of all **acquisitions** of goods and related costs, excluding any VAT, from other **EC Member States** (Box 9)	669 Whole pounds only

Workings

Box 1	£
VAT on sales	2,709.98
Less:VAT on credit notes	(284.50)
	2,425.48

Box 4	£
VAT on purchases	1,422.30
EC Member States acquisitions	117.08
	1,539.38
Less:VAT on credit notes	(163.70)
	1,375.68

Box 6	£
Standard-rated sales	15,485.60
Zero-rated sales	1,497.56
	16,983.16
Less: credit notes	
Standard-rated	(1,625.77)
Zero-rated	(106.59)
	15,250.80

Box 7	£
Standard-rated purchases	8,127.45
Zero-rated purchases	980.57
EC acquisitions	669.04
	9,777.06
Less: credit notes	
Standard-rated	(935.47)
Zero-rated	(80.40)
	8,761.19

WORKBOOK

QUESTIONS

Practice activities - questions

1 Chapter 1 activities

Activity 1

Read the following statements and state whether they are true or false.

1 Output tax must be charged on all sales made by a registered F trader.

2 Registered traders can always recover all their input tax. F

3 VAT is borne by the final consumer. T

4 Registered traders making zero rated supplies cannot recover any input tax. F

Activity 2

A business supplies goods that are a mixture of standard rated and exempt. Which of the following statements is true? Select one answer.

A All of the input VAT can be reclaimed.

B None of the input VAT can be reclaimed.

C All of the input VAT can be reclaimed provided certain de minimis conditions are met. 625   50%

D Some of the input VAT can be reclaimed, in proportion to the different types of supply.

Activity 3

Calculate the amount of VAT at the standard rate which is included in the following VAT inclusive figures.

1 £528.75   7875

2 £5,875   886.72   875

3 £4,230   630

4 £4,794   714

Activity 4

Which of the following is NOT a power of HMRC? Select one answer.

A   Inspecting premises
B   Completing your VAT return
C   Examining records
D   Determining whether certain supplies are liable for VAT

Activity 5

You are given the following information about sales of capital assets in the quarter to 31.12.X1.

Complete the table to show the amount of output tax that must be charged on each item.

Item	Input tax recovered	Sale proceeds (excl VAT) £	Output tax £
Computer	Yes	2,100	367.5
Car	No	10,000	nil
Van	Yes	12,500	2187.5
Motorcycle	Yes	6,760	1183

Activity 6

Scott Ltd provides a car for an employee who uses the car for both private and business use. All running expenses of the car are paid for by the company including fuel. Which one of the following statements is true?

A   There is no effect on VAT.

B   The company can recover all the input tax on the running costs and need take no further action.

C   The company can recover all the input tax on the running costs of the car and must add an amount to output tax determined by a scale charge.

D   The company cannot recover input tax on running costs of the car but must add an amount to output tax determined by a scale charge.

 Activity 7

You are given the following information about purchases and expenses of a manufacturing business in the quarter to 30.6.X1.

Select Yes or No in the final column to show if the input tax on each item can be reclaimed.

Description	Input VAT £	Reclaim input VAT?
Car – for personal use by employee	1,960.00	Yes/No
Customer entertainment	235.50	Yes/No
Staff party	142.70	Yes/No
Office supplies	27.45	Yes/No

Activity 8

You are given the following information about the drawings account of Valerie, a sole trader. Complete the table to show the amount of output tax (if any) that must be accounted for on the drawings.

Description	Original cost £	Replacement cost £	Output VAT £
Goods for own use	500	530	92.75
Cash drawings	1,000	1,000	nil

 Activity 9

When a taxpayer appeals against an HMRC decision they will be offered a choice of an internal review or a referral to the Tax Tribunal.

Which one of the following statements is true?

A   If a taxpayer chooses an internal review they cannot then take their case to the Tax Tribunal if they are dissatisfied with the result of the review.

B   If a taxpayer chooses a review they can still take their case to the Tax Tribunal if dissatisfied with the result of the review.

 Activity 10

Which of the following is the correct definition of a taxable person?

A   A business which is registered for VAT

B   A business which should be registered for VAT

C   A business which is or should be registered for VAT

2 Chapter 2 activities

 Activity 11

You are given the following information about the taxable supplies of four businesses. For each of them select whether they need to register for VAT immediately, or monitor turnover and register later. Tick one box on each line.

		Register now	Monitor and register later
1	A new business with an expected turnover of £70,000 per month for the next 12 months.	✓	
2	An existing business with a total turnover of £65,000 for the last 11 months. Turnover for the next month is not known.		✓
3	An exisitng business with a turnover of £6,000 per month for the last 12 months	✓	
4	An existing business with a turnover of £6,000 per month for the last 6 months which is expected to increase to £7,000 per month for the next 6 months.		✓

Activity 12

Wayne runs three sole trader businesses and is also in partnership with his wife running a fourth business. Each of the businesses has taxable supplies exceeding the VAT registration limit. How many VAT registrations are required?

A   1
B   2
C   3
D   4

 Activity 13

You are given the following information about four traders.

Do the traders **have** to register for VAT? Tick one box on each line.

		Yes	No
1	A trader making only zero rated supplies of £100,000 per year.		✓
2	A trader who has taxable supplies of £80,000 for the last 12 months, but who expects only £60,000 for the next 12 months.		✓
3	A trader who runs two separate businesses making standard rated supplies of £40,000 each.	✓	
4	A trader who runs two separate businesses making standard rated supplies of £60,000 in one business and exempt supplies of £20,000 in the other.		✓

Activity 14

Mark the following statements as true or false. Tick one box on each line

		True	False
1	An unregistered trader can never have a VAT liability to HMRC.		✓
2	A trader making only taxable supplies of £50,000 per year cannot register for VAT.		✓
3	A trader making only exempt supplies of £100,000 per annum must register for VAT.		✓
4	A trader's VAT registration number must be quoted on all their invoices.	✓	
5	A trader whom is already registered must deregister if their supplies fall below the deregistration limit.		✓

 Activity 15

Brown commenced in business on 1 Jan 20X1 making only taxable supplies. His turnover was as follows:

First 6 months to 30.6.20X1   £5,000 per month   30000
Next 12 months to 30.6.20X2   £6,100 per month   73700

1   On which of the following dates does Brown exceed the registration limit of £68,000?

    A   31 December 20X1
    B   31 January 20X2
    C   28 February 20X2
    D   31 March 20X2

2. Select the date by which Brown should notify HMRC that he has exceeded the registration limit.

A 30 December 20X1
B 30 January 20X2
C 2 March 20X2
D 30 March 20X2

 Activity 16

Select one reason why a business making taxable supplies might choose to register voluntarily.

A It would make their prices cheaper to the general public.
B The business would be able to reclaim input VAT.
C Preparation of VAT returns would be optional.

---

3 Chapter 3 activities

 Activity 17

Mark the following statements as true or false. Tick one box on each line

		True	False
1	Traders do not have to supply a VAT invoice unless their customer is VAT registered.	✓	
2	Retailers can issue less detailed VAT invoices if the total amount of the supply, excluding VAT, does not exceed £250.	✗	✓

| 3 | The VAT invoice is used by a customer as their evidence for reclaiming input VAT. | ✓ | |
| 4 | A VAT invoice must be issued to a customer within 30 days of the tax point. | ✓ | |

Activity 18

Calculate the amount of output VAT that should be charged on the following invoices. All goods are standard rated.

Goods pre discount price £	Trade discount	Settlement discount	Output tax £
1,000	10%	2%	154.35
2,000	Nil	5% if paid within 7 days. 2% if paid within 21 days	332.5 343
750	8%	None	120.75

Activity 19

Look at the following list of items. Select by entering the appropriate number whether the items should:

1   Only be shown on a normal detailed VAT invoice or,

2   Shown on both a normal detailed VAT invoice and on a less detailed invoice or,

3   Not be shown on either.

	Item	Number (1, 2, or 3)
A	Identifying number	1
B	Tax point date	2
C	Delivery date	3
D	Total amount of VAT payable	1
E	Customer's registration number	3

 Activity 20

Which of the following statements about proforma invoices are FALSE.

Enter a tick in the final box for each false statement.

		False
A	A proforma invoice IS a valid tax invoice	✓
B	A proforma invoice IS NOT a valid tax invoice	
C	A customer receiving a proforma invoice can use it to reclaim the input tax shown	✓
D	A proforma invoice is really just a demand for payment	

Activity 21

A business issues a sales credit note. What is the effect on output VAT?

A   Output VAT will increase.
B   Output VAT will decrease.
C   Input VAT will increase.
D   Input VAT will decrease.

 Activity 22

In each of the following cases, state the tax point date.

		Tax point
1	Goods delivered to a customer on 15 August, invoice sent out on 20 August and payment received 30 August	20. Aug
2	Proforma invoice issued 3 June, payment received 10 June, goods delivered 30 June with a tax invoice dated on that day	10. Jun
3	Goods delivered to a customer on 4 March, invoice sent out on 25 March and payment received 15 April	4 Mar
4	Invoice sent to a customer on 10 December, goods delivered 18 December and payment received 27 December	10

Activity 23

A VAT registered business receives a £100 non refundable deposit on 19 October from a customer for the supply of goods which are despatched on 25 October. The goods are invoiced on 31 October and the balance of £350 is paid on 10 November. Both amounts are VAT inclusive.

1 What is the tax point for the deposit?

   A   19 October
   B   25 October
   C   31 October
   D   10 November

2 What is the output VAT on the deposit?

   A   £17.50
   B   £14.89

3 What is the tax point for the balance?

   A   19 October
   B   25 October
   C   31 October
   D   10 November

4 What is the output VAT on the balance?

   A   £61.25
   B   £52.12

KAPLAN PUBLISHING

4 Chapter 4 activities

Activity 24

Mark the following statements about the flat rate scheme as true or false. Tick one box on each line

		True	False
1	VAT invoices are not issued to customers.		✓
2	A VAT account need not be kept.		✓
3	Traders using the flat rate scheme can also join the annual accounting scheme.	✓	
4	Traders can join the flat rate scheme if their taxable turnover for the last 12 months is below £225,000.		✓
5	The flat rate scheme percentage varies according to the trade sector of the business.	✓	

Activity 25

A VAT registered business has a year end of 30 June 20X2 and uses the annual accounting scheme.

1 Which one of the following statements is true? (Ignore the extension given to businesses that pay electronically).

A   The whole VAT liability for the year is paid on 31 August 20X2.

B   The VAT liability is paid in nine monthly instalments starting on 31 October 20X1 with a balancing payment on 31 July 20X2.

C   The VAT liability is paid in nine monthly instalments starting on 31 October 20X1 with a balancing payment on 31 August 20X2.

2   The annual VAT return is submitted by which date? (Ignore the extension given to businesses that submit their returns electronically).

A   31 July 20X2

B   31 August 20X2

 Activity 26

Oak Ltd has prepared its VAT return for the quarter ended 30 September.

1   Select which of the following is Oak Ltd's return due date assuming they do not submit electronically

A   14 October

B   31 October

C   7 November

2   What would be the due date for submission of the return if Oak Ltd submitted electronically?

A   14 October

B   31 October

C   7 November

 Activity 27

Which of the following is not an advantage of the flat rate scheme?

A   The business gets a discount of 1% on the flat rate percentage in the first year.

B   VAT returns do not need to be completed.

C   The business does not have to record the VAT charged on individual sales and purchases.

D   The business has easier administration as it does not have to decide which input VAT can be reclaimed and which cannot.

Activity 28

Mark the following statements about the cash accounting scheme as true or false. Tick one box on each line

		True	False
1	VAT invoices are not issued to customers.		✓
2	The scheme gives automatic bad debt relief	✓	
3	Cash accounting is useful for businesses with a high proportion of cash sales		✓
4	If a business adopts cash accounting then their customers cannot reclaim input VAT until they pay their invoices		✓
5	A business cannot join the cash accounting scheme if their VAT returns are not up to date	✓	

Activity 29

In the year ended 31 December 20X1, Pear Ltd has annual sales of £75,000, all of which are standard rated and to the general public. The company incurs standard rated expenses of £6,100 per annum. These figures are VAT exclusive.

1   Select which of the following gives Pear Ltd's liability using the standard method.

   A   £10,261.70
   B   £10,102.71
   Ⓒ   £12,057.50
   D   £12,216.49

2   Select which of the following gives Pear Ltd's VAT liability using the flat rate method assuming a percentage of 8%.

   A   £6,000.00
   Ⓑ   £7,050.00

Activity 30

1   Which one of the following statements is true?

   A   Traders using the standard accounting scheme normally submit their VAT returns every quarter.

   B   Paper VAT returns must be submitted 30 days after the end of the return period.

   C   A trader is always permitted to pay VAT by sending a cheque through the post.

2   What is the annual turnover limit for eligibility to join the annual accounting scheme?

   A   £1,350,000

   B   £1,600,000

3   John's VAT liability for the previous year was £7,200.00. He estimates it will be £7,800.00 this year. He joins the annual accounting scheme and elects to pay by quarterly instalments. What is the size of each instalment?

   A   £1,800.00

   B   £1,950.00

4   Look at the following statements about cash accounting and state which one is false.

   A   Cash accounting is a disadvantage for a business selling zero rated supplies.

   B   VAT invoices need not be sent out.

   C   The key record for determining VAT due is the cash book.

5   Zak is a registered trader using the flat rate scheme with a percentage of 12%. His sales for the quarter are all standard rated and are £75,000 inclusive of VAT.
   What VAT should he pay over for the quarter?

   A   £9,000.00

   B   £10,575.00

5 Chapter 5 activities

 Activity 31

1   Tax avoidance is illegal and tax evasion is legal. TRUE or FALSE?

2   What are the consequences of submitting an incorrect VAT return? Choose ONE answer.

   A   A penalty may be charged and the error must be corrected on the next VAT return.

   B   A penalty may be charged and the error must be corrected by submitting it on form 652.

   C   A penalty will be charged and the way in which the error is corrected depends on its size.

   D   A penalty may be charged and the way in which the error is corrected depends on its size.

3   Tariq finds that he made a net error on an earlier VAT return of £12,400.00. If his turnover for the current quarter is £750,000 how should he correct the error?

   A   By inclusion on his next VAT return

   B   By separate notification on form 652 or by letter.

4   Fill in the blanks in the following statements.

   A surcharge liability notice runs for 12 months after the end of the return period for which the trader is in default.

   Once the surcharge period has started a VAT default occurs when VAT is paid ..late

   A small business with turnover up to 150.... will not be issued a surcharge liability notice on their first default.

   A surcharge liability notice will not be issued if a trader has a reasonable excuse.

Activity 32

You are given the following information about the net errors and turnover of four businesses. For each of them, indicate whether they can correct the error on the next VAT return or whether separate disclosure is required. Tick ONE box on EACH line.

Net error £	Turnover £	Include in VAT return	Separate disclosure
4,500	40,000	√	
12,500	300,000		√
40,000	4,500,000	√	
55,000	6,000,000		√

 Activity 33

Mark the following statements about VAT errors and penalties as true or false. Tick one box on each line

		True	False
1	If a trader fails to register at the correct time they will have to pay over all the VAT they should have charged to customers since the date they should have been registered.	√	
2	If a trader makes an error in a VAT return they will always be charged a penalty.		√
3	A default only occurs if a trader (not a small business), both pays VAT late and submits a VAT return late.		√
4	Surcharge liability notices cover a period of 12 months.	√	

6 Chapter 6 activities

Activity 34

You are a self-employed accounting technician and Duncan Bye, a motor engineer, is one of your clients. He is registered for VAT.

His records for the quarter ended 30 June 20X1 showed the following:

Sales day book

	Gross £	Net £	VAT £
April	7,931.25	6,750.00	1,181.25
May	7,649.25	6,510.00	1,139.25
June	9,682.00	8,240.00	1,442.00
	25,262.50	21,500.00	3,762.50

Purchases day book

	Gross £	Net £	VAT £
April	3,701.25	3,150.00	551.25
May	3,842.25	3,270.00	572.25
June	3,149.00	2,680.00	469.00
	10,692.50	9,100.00	1,592.50

He also gives you some details of petty cash expenditure in the quarter.

	£
Net purchases	75.60
VAT	13.23
	88.83

He informs you that he used some parts on a job to repair his own car. The parts had previously cost him £120 (exclusive of VAT).

Prepare the following VAT form 100 for the period.

VAT due in this period on **sales** and other outputs (Box 1)

VAT due in this period on **acquisitions** from other **EC Member States** (Box 2)

Total VAT due (**the sum of boxes 1 and 2**) (Box 3)

VAT reclaimed in the period on **purchases** and other inputs, including acquisitions from the EC (Box 4)

Net VAT to be paid to HM Revenue & Customs or reclaimed by you (**Difference between boxes 3 and 4**) (Box 5)

Total value of **sales** and all other outputs excluding any VAT. **Include your box 8 figure** (Box 6)

Whole pounds only

Total value of purchases and all other inputs excluding any VAT. **Include your box 9 figure** (Box 7)

Whole pounds only

Total value of all **supplies** of goods and related costs, excluding any VAT, to other **EC Member States** (Box 8)

Whole pounds only

Total value of all **acquisitions** of goods and related costs, excluding any VAT, from other **EC Member States** (Box 9)

Whole pounds only

Activity 35

You are provided with the following summary of Mark Ambrose's books and other information provided by Mark for the quarter ended 30 September 20X1.

MARK AMBROSE

**Summary of day books and petty cash expenditure
Quarter ended 30 September 20X1**

Sales day book

	Work done	VAT	Total
	£	£	£
July	12,900.00	2,257.50	15,157.50
August	13,200.00	2,310.00	15,510.00
September	12,300.00	2,152.50	14,452.50
	38,400.00	6,720.00	45,120.00

Purchase day book

	Net	VAT	Total
	£	£	£
July	5,250.00	918.75	6,168.75
August	5,470.00	957.25	6,427.25
September	5,750.00	1,006.25	6,756.25
	16,470.00	2,882.25	19,352.25

Petty cash expenditure for quarter (VAT inclusive)

July	£105.75	15.75	90
August	£94.00	14	80
September	£117.50	17.5	100
		47.85	270

I have also used some materials from my stock, valued at £500 (exclusive of VAT), to repair my garage roof.

Bad debts list – 30 September 20X1

Date	Customer	Total (including VAT)
30 November 20X0	High Melton Farms	£293.75
3 January 20X1	Concorde Motors	£176.25
4 April 20X1	Bawtry Engineering	£117.50

(handwritten annotations to right of table:)
43.75 250
26.25 150
17.5   100
87.5   500

These have now been written off as bad debts.

Complete boxes 1 to 9 of the VAT return for the quarter ended 30 September 20X1

KAPLAN PUBLISHING

VAT due in this period on **sales** and other outputs (Box 1)

VAT due in this period on **acquisitions** from other **EC Member States** (Box 2)

Total VAT due (**the sum of boxes 1 and 2**) (Box 3)

VAT reclaimed in the period on **purchases** and other inputs, including acquisitions from the EC (Box 4)

Net VAT to be paid to HM Revenue & Customs or reclaimed by you (**Difference between boxes 3 and 4**) (Box 5)

Total value of **sales** and all other outputs excluding any VAT. **Include your box 8 figure** (Box 6)

Whole pounds only

Total value of purchases and all other inputs excluding any VAT. **Include your box 9 figure** (Box 7)

Whole pounds only

Total value of all **supplies** of goods and related costs, excluding any VAT, to other **EC Member States** (Box 8)

Whole pounds only

Total value of all **acquisitions** of goods and related costs, excluding any VAT, from other **EC Member States** (Box 9)

Whole pounds only

Activity 36

The following accounts have been extracted from a company's ledgers

Date		Dr £	Cr £
Sales: UK			
30.6.X1	Sales day book		60,500
31.7.X1	Sales day book		89,510
31.8 X1	Sales day book		70,400
Sales: Export EC			
30.6.X1	Sales day book		15,150
31.7.X1	Sales day book		20,580
31.8 X1	Sales day book		17,890
Sales: Exports non EC			
30.6.X1	Sales day book		8,500
31.7.X1	Sales day book		7,450
31.8 X1	Sales day book		10,100
Purchases:UK			
30.6.X1	Purchases day book	34,600	
31.7.X1	Purchases day book	31,590	
31.8 X1	Purchases day book	33,670	
VAT: Output Tax			
30.6.X1	Sales day book		10,587.50
31.7.X1	Sales day book		15,664.25
31.8 X1	Sales day book		12,320.00
VAT: Input tax			
30.6.X1	Purchases day book	6,055.00	
31.7.X1	Purchases day book	5,528.25	
31.8 X1	Purchases day book	5,892.25	

Bad debt relief on a sales invoice for £5,875 including VAT is to be claimed this quarter.

The business overstated output VAT of £2,350 in the previous quarter and this must be corrected.

Prepare the following VAT form 100 for the period. The company submits and pays electronically.

VAT due in this period on **sales** and other outputs (Box 1)

VAT due in this period on **acquisitions** from other **EC Member States** (Box 2)

Total VAT due (**the sum of boxes 1 and 2**) (Box 3)

VAT reclaimed in the period on **purchases** and other inputs, including acquisitions from the EC (Box 4)

Net VAT to be paid to HM Revenue & Customs or reclaimed by you (**Difference between boxes 3 and 4**) (Box 5)

Total value of **sales** and all other outputs excluding any VAT. **Include your box 8 figure** (Box 6)

Whole pounds only

Total value of purchases and all other inputs excluding any VAT. **Include your box 9 figure** (Box 7)

Whole pounds only

Total value of all **supplies** of goods and related costs, excluding any VAT, to other **EC Member States** (Box 8)

Whole pounds only

Total value of all **acquisitions** of goods and related costs, excluding any VAT, from other **EC Member States** (Box 9)

Whole pounds only

Activity 37

Assume you are a junior accountant working in the company included in Activity 36. Draft a suitable short email to the financial accountant of the company advising him that the form has been completed and the date the tax is due.

Assume today's date is 12 September 20X1.

 Activity 38

Warhorse Ltd runs a UK business selling standard rated horse-riding accessories. The company imports some items from overseas, both from other EC countries and from outside the EC. The VAT rate is 17.5%.

In the quarter ended 30 June 20X2 the details of purchases are as follows:

	£
Purchases from UK businesses	31,250
Purchases from EC registered businesses	7,650
Purchases from outside the EC	15,850

All these figures exclude VAT.

What are the figures to include in Boxes 2, 4, 7 and 9?

Activity 39

You are required to complete a VAT return for Coleman Limited in respect of the quarter ended 31 December 20X8. You are given the following information to assist you in this task:

1   Of the external sales of £916,000 made during the quarter ended 31 December 20X8, a total of £65,000 relates to exports to EU countries. The remainder of this quarter's sales was of standard rated sales to UK customers. All sales figures given exclude VAT.

2   Total purchases by the company in the quarter amounted to £310,000 of standard-rated inputs, and £23,000 of zero-rated inputs (both figures stated are exclusive of VAT). All of these purchases were from within the UK.

3   The sales figures for October 20X8 include an invoice for standard-rated goods with a value, excluding VAT, of £3,200. These goods were actually despatched in September 20X8 and should have been accounted for in the VAT return for the previous quarter, but were omitted in error.

4   A debt of £611, inclusive of VAT, was written off as bad during the month of December 20X8. The related sale was made in February 20X8. Bad debt relief is now to be claimed.

Preparc the following VAT form 100 for the period. The company submits and pays electronically.

VAT due in this period on **sales** and other outputs (Box 1)

VAT due in this period on **acquisitions** from other **EC Member States** (Box 2)

Total VAT due (**the sum of boxes 1 and 2**) (Box 3)

VAT reclaimed in the period on **purchases** and other inputs, including acquisitions from the EC (Box 4)

Net VAT to be paid to HM Revenue & Customs or reclaimed by you (**Difference between boxes 3 and 4**) (Box 5)

Total value of **sales** and all other outputs excluding any VAT. **Include your box 8 figure** (Box 6)

Whole pounds only

Total value of purchases and all other inputs excluding any VAT. **Include your box 9 figure** (Box 7)

Whole pounds only

Total value of all **supplies** of goods and related costs, excluding any VAT, to other **EC Member States** (Box 8)

Whole pounds only

Total value of all **acquisitions** of goods and related costs, excluding any VAT, from other **EC Member States** (Box 9)

Whole pounds only

KAPLAN PUBLISHING

Activity 40

Refer to the three invoices set out below which have been received from suppliers during March 20X8. No entries have yet been made in Hoddle Ltd's books of account in respect of these 3 documents.

You are required to state whether these are valid VAT tax invoices and how much input tax (if any) can be claimed in respect of these.

Engineering Supplies Limited

Haddlefield Road, Blaysley, CG6 6AW
Tel/Fax: 01376 44531

Hoddle Limited   **SALES INVOICE NO:** 2155
22 Formguard Street
Pexley
PY6 3QW

Date: 27 March 20X8

VAT omitted in error from invoice no 2139
dated 15 March 20X8   £

£2,667.30 @ 17.5%   466.77

Total due   466.77
                                            ——————

Terms: net 30 days

VAT registration: 318 1827 58

Alpha Stationery

Aindsale Centre, Mexton, EV1 4DF
Telephone: 01392 43215

26 March 20X8

1 box transparent folders : red

Total incl VAT @ 17.5%   14.84
Amount tendered   20.00
Change   5.16

VAT registration: 356 7612 33

JAMIESON & CO

Jamieson House, Baines Road, Gresham, GM7 2PQ
Telephone: 01677 35567   Fax: 01677 57640

PROFORMA SALES

INVOICE

VAT registration: 412 7553 67

Hoddle Limited
22 Formguard Street
Pexley
PY6 3QW

For professional services in connection with debt collection

	£
Our fees	350.00
VAT	61.25
Total due	411.25

A VAT invoice will be submitted when the total due is paid in full.

	Valid VAT invoice	Input tax (£)
Engineering Supplies Ltd	YES/NO	
Alpha Stationery	YES/NO	
Jamieson and Co	YES/NO	

Activity 41

You are given the following summaries of the sales and purchases daybooks, the cash book and the petty cash book of Defoe Ltd

Use this information to complete the VAT return for the quarter ended 31 March 20X8.

DEFOE LIMITED : SALES DAY BOOK SUMMARY

JANUARY TO MARCH 20X8

	JAN £	FEB £	MAR £	TOTAL £
UK: ZERO-RATED	20,091.12	22,397.00	23,018.55	65,506.67
UK: STANDARD-RATED	15,682.30	12,914.03	15,632.98	44,229.31
OTHER EU	874.12	4,992.66	5,003.82	10,870.60
VAT	2,744.40	2,259.95	2,735.77	7,740.12
TOTAL	39,391.94	42,563.64	46,391.12	128,346.70

DEFOE LIMITED : PURCHASES DAY BOOK SUMMARY

JANUARY TO MARCH 20X8

	JAN £	FEB £	MAR £	TOTAL £
PURCHASES	14,532.11	20,914.33	15,461.77	50,908.21
DISTRIBUTION EXPENSES	4,229.04	3,761.20	5,221.43	13,211.67
ADMIN EXPENSES	5,123.08	2,871.45	3,681.62	11,676.15
OTHER EXPENSES	1,231.00	1,154.99	997.65	3,383.64
VAT	4,027.97	4,543.22	4,119.34	12,690.53
TOTAL	29,143.20	33,245.19	29,481.81	91,870.20

DEFOE LIMITED : CASH BOOK SUMMARY

JANUARY TO MARCH 20X8

	JAN £	FEB £	MAR £	TOTAL £
PAYMENTS:				
TO CREDITORS	12,901.37	15,312.70	18,712.44	46,926.51
TO PETTY CASH	601.40	555.08	623.81	1,780.29
WAGES/SALARIES	5,882.18	6,017.98	6,114.31	18,014.47
TOTAL	19,384.95	21,885.76	25,450.56	66,721.27
RECEIPTS:				
VAT FROM HMRC	2,998.01			2,998.01
FROM CUSTOMERS	29,312.44	34,216.08	36,108.77	99,637.29
TOTAL	32,310.45	34,216.08	36,108.77	102,635.30

DEFOE LIMITED : PETTY CASH BOOK SUMMARY

JANUARY TO MARCH 20X8

	JAN £	FEB £	MAR £	TOTAL £
PAYMENTS:				
STATIONERY	213.85	80.12	237.58	531.55
TRAVEL	87.34	76.50	102.70	266.54
OFFICE EXPENSES	213.66	324.08	199.51	737.25
VAT	86.55	74.38	84.02	244.95
TOTAL	601.40	555.08	623.81	1,780.29
RECEIPTS:				
FROM CASH BOOK	601.40	555.08	623.81	1,780.29

Blank VAT return for completion

VAT due in this period on **sales** and other outputs (Box 1)

VAT due in this period on **acquisitions** from other **EC Member States** (Box 2)

Total VAT due (**the sum of boxes 1 and 2**) (Box 3)

VAT reclaimed in the period on **purchases** and other inputs, including acquisitions from the EC (Box 4)

Net VAT to be paid to HM Revenue & Customs or reclaimed by you (**Difference between boxes 3 and 4**) (Box 5)

Total value of **sales** and all other outputs excluding any VAT. **Include your box 8 figure** (Box 6)

Whole pounds only

Total value of purchases and all other inputs excluding any VAT. **Include your box 9 figure** (Box 7)

Whole pounds only

Total value of all **supplies** of goods and related costs, excluding any VAT, to other **EC Member States** (Box 8)

Whole pounds only

Total value of all **acquisitions** of goods and related costs, excluding any VAT, from other **EC Member States** (Box 9)

Whole pounds only

ANSWERS

Practice activities – answers

1 Chapter 1 activities - answers

Activity 1

1 False – some sales may be exempt.

2 False – some input tax is blocked and cannot be reclaimed. Also traders making some exempt supplies may not be able to recover all their input tax.

3 True

4 False – zero rated supplies are taxable supplies so VAT can be recovered.

Activity 2

C is the correct answer. A partially exempt business has to apportion input tax in proportion to the levels of taxable and exempt supplies. However, if the exempt input tax is below the de minimis limit the whole of the input tax can be recovered.

Activity 3

1 £78.75

2 £875.00

3 £630.00

4 £714.00

Activity 4

B is the correct answer. A, C and D are all powers of HMRC.

 Activity 5

Computer	£367.50 (£2,100 × 17.5%)
Car	Nil – sale of a car on which the input tax was not recoverable is an exempt supply.
Van	£2,187.50 (£12,500 × 17.5%)
Motorcycle	£1,183.00 (£6,760 × 17.5%)

 Activity 6

C is the correct answer. When a business supplies a car to an employee who uses the car at least partly privately, and pays for fuel, then the business can recover the input VAT on running costs including petrol. However, they must account for output tax determined by a table of scale charges.

 Activity 7

Car – No reclaim of input tax if there is some private use of the car
Customer entertainment – No reclaim of input tax
Staff party – Yes, input tax is recoverable
Office supplies – Yes, input tax is recoverable

 Activity 8

Output VAT on drawings of goods is based on the replacement cost.
£530 × 17.5% = £92.75

No output VAT is due on cash drawings.

Activity 9

B is the correct answer.

 Activity 10

C is the correct answer.

2 Chapter 2 activities - answers

 Activity 11

1   Register now – turnover is expected to exceed the registration limit in the next 30 days.

2   Monitor and register later – turnover for the period to date does not exceed the registration limit.

3   Register now – turnover has exceeded the registration limit in the last 12 months.

4   Monitor and register later – turnover has not exceeded the limit.

 Activity 12

B   2 registrations are needed. One to cover all of Wayne's sole trader businesses and one to cover the partnership with his wife.

Activity 13

1 No – businesses that only make zero rated supplies need not register for VAT.

2 No – if a business exceeds the registration limit it need not register if taxable turnover in the next 12 months will be below the deregistration threshold.

3 Yes – the taxable turnover of all a trader's sole trader businesses are aggregated to determine whether the business has exceeded the VAT threshold.

4 No – exempt supplies are not taken into account for registration.

 Activity 14

1 False – if a trader fails to register when they should, then they can be asked to pay over all the output VAT they should have charged.

2 False – traders making taxable supplies can register voluntarily.

3 False – traders making only exempt supplies cannot register for VAT.

4 True – the VAT registration number must be shown on all invoices.

5 False – traders only have to deregister if they cease to make taxable supplies. If their supplies fall below the deregistration limit they can choose to deregister.

 Activity 15

1 C –Taxable turnover for the first 12 months to 31 December is £66,600, to 31 January £67,700 and to 28 February £68,800.

2 D – Traders must notify HMRC within 30 days of exceeding the limit.

Activity 16

B is the correct answer.

A is incorrect as the public would have to pay VAT which they could not recover. C is incorrect as VAT returns would have to be completed.

3   Chapter 3 activities - answers

Activity 17

1   True – it is only compulsory to issue VAT invoices to registered traders.
2   False – the £250 is VAT inclusive .
3   True – VAT invoices form the evidence for the reclaim of input tax.
4   True

Activity 18

VAT must be charged on the price payable after discount.

£154.35 (£1,000 – 10% of £1,000 = £900 – 2% of £900) × 17.5%

£332.50 (£2,000 – 5% of £2,000) × 17.5%

£120.75 (£750 – 8% of £750) × 17.5%

Activity 19

A   1
B   2
C   3
D   1
E   3

Activity 20

A and C are false. A proforma invoice is NOT a valid tax invoice, nor is it evidence that allows the customer to reclaim input tax.

 Activity 21

B is the correct answer.

 Activity 22

1   20 August. The invoice is raised within 14 days of the delivery date (the basic tax point) and hence a later tax point is created.

2   10 June. The issue of the proforma invoice is ignored so the receipt of payment is the tax point.

3   4 March. The invoice is raised more than 14 days after the delivery date so the tax point stays on the delivery date.

4   10 December. The goods are invoiced before delivery so this creates an earlier tax point.

Activity 23

1   A   Receipt of cash on 19 October creates a tax point

2   B   £100 is VAT inclusive so the VAT element is £14.89 (£100 × 7/47)

3   C   The goods are invoiced within 14 days of delivery so a later tax point is created

4   B   £350 is VAT inclusive so the VAT element is £52.12 (£350 × 7/47)

4 Chapter 4 activities - answers

Activity 24

1   False – VAT invoices must still be supplied to customers.

2   False – A VAT account must still be kept.

3   True – It is possible to be in the flat rate and the annual accounting scheme .

4   False – the limit to join the scheme is £150,000.

5   True – The flat rate percentage is determined by your trade sector.

Activity 25

1   C   This is how the annual accounting scheme payments are made.

2   B   31 August 20X2 – two months after the year end.

Activity 26

1   B   31 October – one month after the end of the quarter.

2   C   7 November – 7 extra days are given for online submissions.

Activity 27

B   VAT returns must still be completed.

Activity 28

1   False – VAT invoices must still be issued.

2   True – this is one of the advantages of the scheme.

3   False – business with a high level of cash sales do not benefit from cash accounting.

4   False – cash accounting does not affect customers.

5   True – this is one of the conditions for joining the scheme.

 Activity 29

1   C   (£75,000 – £6,100) × 17.5%

2   B   (£75,000 + 17.5% of £75,000) × 8%. The percentage must be applied to the VAT inclusive figure.

 Activity 30

1   A is true. B is false as the time limit is 1 month. C is false as traders cannot pay by post if they submit electronic returns.

2   A   £1,350,000

3   A   £1,800.00 (£7,200 / 4)

4   B is false. A and C are true.

5   A   £9,000.00 (£75,000 × 12%)

5 Chapter 5 activities - answers

 Activity 31

1 FALSE – it is the other way round. Avoidance is legal and evasion is illegal.

2 D – a penalty may be charged and the way in which the error is corrected depends on its size.

3 B – the error is between £10,000 and £50,000 but is more than 1% of turnover, hence it must be separately disclosed.

4 A surcharge liability notice runs for …*12*.. months after the end of the return period for which the trader is in default.

Once the surcharge period has started a VAT default occurs when VAT is paid …*late*..

A small business with turnover up to …*£150,000*….. will not be issued a surcharge liability notice on their first default.

A surcharge liability notice will not be issued if a trader has a …*reasonable*…excuse.

Activity 32

Include in VAT return. The error is less than £10,000.

Separate disclosure. The error is over £10,000 and more than 1% of turnover.

Include in VAT return. The error is between £10,000 and £50,000 and less than 1% of turnover.

Separate disclosure. The error is more than £50,000

 Activity 33

1   True

2   False – they will not ALWAYS be charged a penalty.

3   False – a default occurs when a return is submitted late OR a late payment made.

4   True

KAPLAN PUBLISHING

6 Chapter 6 activities - answers

Activity 34

VAT due in this period on sales and other outputs (Box 1)	3,783.50 ✓
VAT due in this period on acquisitions from other EC Member States (Box 2)	0.00
Total VAT due (the sum of boxes 1 and 2) (Box 3)	3,783.50 ✓
VAT reclaimed in the period on purchases and other inputs, including acquisitions from the EC (Box 4)	1,605.73 ✓
Net VAT to be paid to HM Revenue & Customs or reclaimed by you (Difference between boxes 3 and 4) (Box 5)	2,177.77 ✓
Total value of sales and all other outputs excluding any VAT. Include your box 8 figure (Box 6)	21,620 ✓
	Whole pounds only
Total value of purchases and all other inputs excluding any VAT. Include your box 9 figure (Box 7)	9,176 ✓
	Whole pounds only
Total value of all supplies of goods and related costs, excluding any VAT, to other EC Member States (Box 8)	0
	Whole pounds only

Total value of all acquisitions of goods and related costs, excluding any VAT, from other EC Member States (Box 9)

	0

Whole pounds only

Workings for VAT return

		£
Box 1:	From SDB	3,762.50
	Goods for own use	21.00*
		3,783.50

* £120 × 17.5% = £21

		£
Box 4:	From PDB	1,592.50
	Petty cash	13.23
		1,605.73

		£
Box 6:	From SDB	21,500
	Goods for own use	120
		21,620

		£
Box 7:	From PDB	9,100
	Petty cash (£75.60 rounded up)	76
		9,176

Activity 35

VAT due in this period on sales and other outputs (Box 1)	6,807.50
VAT due in this period on acquisitions from other EC Member States (Box 2)	0.00
Total VAT due (the sum of boxes 1 and 2) (Box 3)	6,807.50
VAT reclaimed in the period on purchases and other inputs, including acquisitions from the EC (Box 4)	2,999.50
Net VAT to be paid to HM Revenue & Customs or reclaimed by you (Difference between boxes 3 and 4) (Box 5)	3,808.00
Total value of sales and all other outputs excluding any VAT. Include your box 8 figure (Box 6)	38,900
	Whole pounds only
Total value of purchases and all other inputs excluding any VAT. Include your box 9 figure (Box 7)	16,740
	Whole pounds only
Total value of all supplies of goods and related costs, excluding any VAT, to other EC Member States (Box 8)	0
	Whole pounds only
Total value of all acquisitions of goods and related costs, excluding any VAT, from other EC Member States (Box 9)	0
	Whole pounds only

Workings for VAT return

		£
Box 1:	From SDB	6,720.00
	Goods for own use	87.50
		_____
		6,807.50
		_____

VAT on goods for own use = £500 × 17.5% = £87.50

		£
Box 4:	From PDB	2,882.25
	Petty cash	47.25
	Bad debts	70.00
		_____
		2,999.50
		_____

Total petty cash expenditure = £(105.75 + 94.00 + 117.50) = £317.25

VAT on £317.25 = 17.5/117.5 × £317.25 = £47.25

Bad debts more than six months old = £(293.75 + 176.25) = £470

VAT on £470 = 17.5/117.5 × £470 = £70

Activity 36

VAT due in this period on sales and other outputs (Box 1)	38,571.75
VAT due in this period on acquisitions from other EC Member States (Box 2)	0.00
Total VAT due (the sum of boxes 1 and 2) (Box 3)	38,571.75
VAT reclaimed in the period on purchases and other inputs, including acquisitions from the EC (Box 4)	20,700.50
Net VAT to be paid to HM Revenue & Customs or reclaimed by you (Difference between boxes 3 and 4) (Box 5)	17,871.25
Total value of sales and all other outputs excluding any VAT. Include your box 8 figure (Box 6)	300,080
	Whole pounds only
Total value of purchases and all other inputs excluding any VAT. Include your box 9 figure (Box 7)	99,860
	Whole pounds only
Total value of all supplies of goods and related costs, excluding any VAT, to other EC Member States (Box 8)	53,620
	Whole pounds only
Total value of all acquisitions of goods and related costs, excluding any VAT, from other EC Member States (Box 9)	0
	Whole pounds only

Workings for VAT return

£

Box 1: From VAT account – output tax
(£10,587.50 + £15,664.25 + £12,320.00)   38,571.75

£

Box 4: From VAT account – input tax
(£6,055.00 + £5,528.25 + £5,892.25)   17,475.50

Bad debts (£5,875 × 17.5/117.5)   875.00

Add: VAT error   2,350.00

20,700.50

Box 6: Sales: UK
(£60,500 + £89,510 + £70,400)   220,410

Sales: Export EC
(£15,150 + £20,580 + £17,890)   53,620

Sales: Export non EC
(£8,500 + £7,450 + £10,100)   26,050

300,080

Box 7: Purchases
(£34,600 + £31,590 + £33,670)   99,860

Activity 37

To: Financial Accountant

From: Junior Accountant

Date: 12 September 20X1

Subject: VAT return for the quarter ended 31 August 20X1

I have completed the return for this period.

The VAT due is £17,871.25. The return must be submitted online by 7 October 20X1 and the VAT paid electronically by the same date.

Activity 38

		£
Box 2	VAT on acquisitions from other EC countries	
	17.5% × £7,650	1,338.75
Box 4	VAT reclaimed	
	17.5% × (£31,250 + £7,650 + £15,850)	9,581.25
Box 7	Total purchases	
	(£31,250 + £7,650 + £15,850)	54,750
Box 9	Purchases from other EC countries	7,650

Activity 39

VAT due in this period on sales and other outputs (Box 1)	148,925.00
VAT due in this period on acquisitions from other EC Member States (Box 2)	0.00
Total VAT due (the sum of boxes 1 and 2) (Box 3)	148,925.00
VAT reclaimed in the period on purchases and other inputs, including acquisitions from the EC (Box 4)	54,341.00
Net VAT to be paid to HM Revenue & Customs or reclaimed by you (Difference between boxes 3 and 4) (Box 5)	94,584.00
Total value of sales and all other outputs excluding any VAT. Include your box 8 figure (Box 6)	916,000
	Whole pounds only
Total value of purchases and all other inputs excluding any VAT. Include your box 9 figure (Box 7)	333,000
	Whole pounds only
Total value of all supplies of goods and related costs, excluding any VAT, to other EC Member States (Box 8)	65,000
	Whole pounds only
Total value of all acquisitions of goods and related costs, excluding any VAT, from other EC Member States (Box 9)	0
	Whole pounds only

Workings for VAT return

		£
Box 1:	External sales	916,000
	Less: Exports to EU countries (zero rated)	(65,000)
	Standard rated sales	851,000
	Output VAT (£851,000 × 17.5%)	148,925.00

		£
Box 4:	VAT on standard rated purchases (£310,000 × 17.5%)	54,250.00
	Bad debt relief (£611 × 17.5/117.5)	91.00
		54,341.00

		£
Box 7:	Standard rated inputs	310,000
	Zero rated inputs	23,000
		333,000

Note that the error does not need to be corrected separately. The error is that output tax in the previous quarter was understated because a sales invoice was left out. The value of the error is below £10,000 so it can be corrected on this period's return. It has already been included in the total of outputs and hence output tax for this quarter, so does not need to be included again.

Activity 40

Engineering Supplies Ltd – this invoice is a valid VAT invoice which should be processed as a March input. The input VAT of £466.77 can be reclaimed in the quarter to 31 March 20X8.

Alpha Stationery – this is a less detailed VAT invoice which should also be processed as a March input. The VAT of £2.21 (£14.84 × 17.5/117.5) can be reclaimed in the quarter to 31 March 20X8.

Jamieson and Co – this is a proforma invoice so cannot be treated as a March input. The VAT cannot be reclaimed until a valid VAT invoice is received.

Activity 41

Defoe Ltd – VAT return for the quarter ended 31 March 20X8

VAT due in this period on sales and other outputs (Box 1)	7,740.12
VAT due in this period on acquisitions from other EC Member States (Box 2)	0.00
Total VAT due (the sum of boxes 1 and 2) (Box 3)	7,740.12
VAT reclaimed in the period on purchases and other inputs, including acquisitions from the EC (Box 4)	12,935.48
Net VAT to be paid to HM Revenue & Customs or reclaimed by you (Difference between boxes 3 and 4) (Box 5)	–5,195.36
Total value of sales and all other outputs excluding any VAT. Include your box 8 figure (Box 6)	120,607
	Whole pounds only
Total value of purchases and all other inputs excluding any VAT. Include your box 9 figure (Box 7)	80,715
	Whole pounds only
Total value of all supplies of goods and related costs, excluding any VAT, to other EC Member States (Box 8)	10,871
	Whole pounds only
Total value of all acquisitions of goods and related costs, excluding any VAT, from other EC Member States (Box 9)	0
	Whole pounds only

Workings for VAT return

		£
Box 4:	From Purchase day book	12,690.53
	From Petty cash book	244.95
		12,935.48
Box 6:	Total from sales day book	128,346.70
	Less: VAT included	(7,740.12)
		120,606.58
Box 7:	Purchase day book total	91,870.20
	Less: VAT included	(12,690.53)
	Petty cash book total	1,780.29
	Less: VAT included	(244.95)
		80,715.01

INDEX